The Legend of

The Legend of Pfizer

Jeffrey L. Rodengen

For Fred Kiekhaefer,

*whose trust and friendship have always
been the perfect prescription.*

Also by Jeff Rodengen

The Legend of Chris-Craft

*IRON FIST: The Lives
of Carl Kiekhaefer*

*Evinrude-Johnson and
The Legend of OMC*

*Serving The Silent Service:
The Legend of Electric Boat*

The Legend of Dr Pepper/Seven-Up

The Legend of Honeywell

The Legend of Briggs & Stratton

The Legend of Ingersoll-Rand

The MicroAge Way

*The Legend of Stanley:
150 Years of The Stanley Works*

The Legend of Halliburton

The Legend of York International

The Legend of Nucor Corporation

*The Legend of Goodyear:
The First 100 Years*

The Legend of AMP

The Legend of Cessna

The Legend of VF Corporation

The Spirit of AMD

The Legend of Rowan

*New Horizons:
The Evolution of Ashland Inc.*

The History of American Standard

The Legend of Mercury Marine

The Legend of Federal-Mogul

*Against the Odds:
Inter-Tel—The First 30 Years*

Publisher's Cataloging in Publication

Rodengen, Jeffrey L.
   The legend of Pfizer /Jeffrey L. Rodengen.
   p. cm.
   Includes bibliographical references and index.
   ISBN 0-945903-37-5

   1. Pfizer Inc 2. Pharmaceutical industry — United States.
I. Title

   HD9666.9.P44R64 1998   338.7'61'61519'0973
                                 QBI97-40431

Write Stuff Syndicate, Inc.

1001 South Andrews Avenue, Second Floor • Fort Lauderdale, FL 33316
1-800-900-Book (1-800-900-2665) • (954) 462-6657

Library of Congress Catalog Card Number 96-61247
ISBN 0-945903-37-5

Completely produced in the United States of America
10 9 8 7 6 5 4 3 2 1

All trademarks in this publication are or have been used by Pfizer Inc with the exception of the following: Aricept is a trademark of Eisai Co., Ltd.; Celebrex is a trademark of G.D. Searle & Co., a division of Monsanto Company; Lipitor is a trademark of Warner-Lambert Company.

TABLE OF CONTENTS

Foreword vi
Acknowledgments viii

SECTION I

Chapter I   The Enterprise Begins 12
Chapter II   A New Leader Takes Command. 22
Chapter III   The War Years 28
Chapter IV   "SUCIAC" Spells Success 34
Chapter V   The Depression Years 42

SECTION II

Chapter VI   The Magic Bullet 52
Chapter VII   Perfecting the Process 58
Chapter VIII   New Plants and New Markets 68
Chapter IX   Conquering New Frontiers 78
Chapter X   Pfizer in Transition .92

SECTION III

Chapter XI   The Age of Research 106
Chapter XII   The Pipeline 118
Chapter XIII   The Triumvirate 128
Chapter XIV   Pfizer in Focus: The Steere Years 134

Pfizer's Gallery of Leaders 152
Bibliography 154
Index 156

FOREWORD

by
William C. Steere, Jr.
Chairman of the Board and Chief Executive Officer, Pfizer Inc

NINETEEN NINETY-NINE marks Pfizer's 150th year of operation. That in itself is a huge achievement. There are few companies in the United States — or in the world — that have existed for a century and a half. Even fewer have kept the same name and remained in their original field.

When we opened our doors in Brooklyn in 1849, Pfizer had one product and two employees. Stagecoaches provided the fastest transportation on land and steamboats were all the rage on the rivers.

Medicine as we know it today was in its infancy. Diphtheria, typhoid, tuberculosis, and pneumonia took a terrible toll on people of all ages. Doctors had few remedies at their disposal and often could do little to ease patients' suffering, much less cure their illnesses.

Fortunately, the situation has improved tremendously today. Many diseases — such as smallpox, which once annihilated entire populations — have been eradicated. Others that used to be fatal can now be cured. The incidence of still others, like polio, which often led to permanent debility and disfigurement, has been greatly reduced.

Pfizer helped to achieve many of these breakthroughs. We've grown from a family business in Brooklyn into a global enterprise that employs nearly 50,000 people on six continents. We manufacture our products in 35 countries and sell them in more than 150. But our most important achievement is this one: In virtually every corner of the world, at every hour of the day and night, millions of people are benefiting from Pfizer medicines.

Ours is a history of medical accomplishment, humanitarian commitment, and financial achievement. But most of all, it's a history of protecting, saving, and enhancing lives.

In the 19th century, our medicines fought internal parasites and treated soldiers on the field of combat in the Civil War. In the 20th century, Pfizer was the first company to successfully mass-produce penicillin. In the 1940s and 1950s, our discoveries helped to usher in the "Age of Antibiotics." And in the 1960s, we helped to eradicate polio in the United States.

Since then, we've pioneered effective treatments for ailments ranging from diabetes and depression to arthritis, heart disease, and life-threatening infections.

The history of Pfizer is the story of a great humanitarian enterprise, of great science, impressive commitment, and remarkable people. Everything our company has achieved always comes back to Pfizer's outstanding people and to their commitment to the Pfizer values.

These eight values — integrity, respect for people, customer focus, performance, innovation, leadership, teamwork, and community — have played a key role in Pfizer's success. And I believe that they will provide a firm foundation for our future prosperity.

But at Pfizer, our goal is not only preeminence, it is also performance with integrity. Our aim is not sheer novelty, but innovation guided by respect for people, focus on our customers, and

service to the community. Our objective is not only to be first in rank, but also to be first in excellence and to exemplify the best leadership and teamwork in the industry.

At Pfizer, we recognize that we've been given a great legacy. We revere the men and women on whose outstanding work and character we build. We are grateful for the inheritance they have entrusted to us. But most of all, we are determined to add to that legacy. We will do everything we can so that 150 years from now, those who come after us will be able to say, as we can today, that the story of Pfizer is not only a great history but also a history of greatness.

ACKNOWLEDGMENTS

RESEARCHING, WRITING, AND publishing *The Legend of Pfizer* would not have been possible without the effort and guidance of a great many individuals, both inside and outside Pfizer.

A very special thanks goes to the members of the Corporate Management Committee, whose support was critical to the book. I'm especially indebted to William C. Steere, Jr., chairman of the board and chief executive officer, who took time from his busy schedule to contribute. I would also like to extend my gratitude to Henry A. McKinnell, Ph.D., president and chief operating officer, president Pfizer Pharmaceuticals Group; John F. Niblack, Ph.D., vice chairman of the board; C.L. Clemente, executive vice president, Corporate Affairs, secretary and corporate counsel; Paul S. Miller, executive vice president, general counsel; William J. Robison, executive vice president, Corporate Employee Resources; David L. Shedlarz, executive vice president and chief financial officer; Karen L. Katen, executive vice president, Pfizer Pharmaceuticals Group and president, U.S. Pharmaceuticals; and George M. Milne, Jr., Ph.D., senior vice president, president, Central Research.

I'd also like to extend special thanks to retired chairman and CEO Edmund T. Pratt, Jr., and to retired and current senior managers, including: Alex Bachmann, Brian Barrett, Edward Bessey, Barry Bloom, M. Kenneth Bowler, Peter Brandt, Bruce Ellig, George Forcier, Terence Gallagher, P. Nigel Gray, Gary Jortner, J. Patrick Kelly, Alan Levin, Brower Merriam, Robert Niemeth, Herbert Ryan, Craig Saxton, Mohand Sidi Said, Frederick Telling, and Jean-Paul Vallès.

Special tribute also goes to the three people who have been closely involved with this project since it first began several years ago, and whose time, talents, and efforts have been invaluable: Elaine Williams-Hunt, Carson Daly, and Jeffrey Brand. In addition, I would like to give special recognition to a number of others whose support was critical to the book's successful completion: Joseph Lombardino, Rick Luftglass, Ron Aldridge, Timothy Goodman, and Denise Johnson.

Thanks also go to the many people who contributed in ways too numerous to describe. They include: Linda Abels, Irene Bernhard, Barbara Breen, Michael Bright, Bob Brown, Erlene Brown, John Campbell, Daniel Casse, Francine Colby, Greg Cowles, Peter Davenport, Vincent DeGennaro, Tom DeLong, Laura Devlin, Bentley Elliot, Theresa Farley, Kim Frawley, Diane Garbato, Anna Gasner, Alex Goudie, Kate Gough, Howard Haag, Chuck Hardwick, Leslie Harr, Janet Hecken, Quentin Heim, Richard Hinman, Michael Hodin, Marianne Houghtaling, Ray Jordan, John Keenan, Kim Kershaw, Jay Kosminsky, Elyse Locurto, Marina Mia, Robert Muller, Loretta Parker, Keith Paulsen, Alan Proctor,

Ellen Rochford, Nancy Rosa, Tena Rufo, Helen Suarez, Ken Taksen, Claudia Turner, Cathy Vongas, Willard Welch, and Edward Wiseman.

I'd like to thank the H.L.C. Group and Ogilvy PR Worldwide for their generous contribution of images and graphics for use in the book.

I'd also like to thank Carol Conn, my dedicated research assistant who conducted much of the archival research and assembled the first narrative timeline.

And finally, a very special word of thanks to the dedicated staff at Write Stuff. Proofreaders Bonnie Freeman and Terry Bridgewater and transcriptionist Mary Aaron worked quickly and efficiently.

Indexer Erika Orloff assembled the comprehensive index. Particular gratitude goes to principal editor, Jon VanZile; Alex Lieber, executive editor; Melody Maysonet, associate editor; Sandy Cruz, senior art director; Jill Apolinario, Barry Carmichael, Rachelle Donley, and Kyle Newton, art directors; Fred Moll, production manager; Colleen Azcona and Jill Thomas, assistants to the author; Marianne Roberts, office manager; Christopher Frosch, marketing and sales manager; Mike Monahan director of sales, marketing and promotion; Bonnie Bratton, director of marketing; Rafael Santiago, logistics specialist; and Karine Rodengen, project coordinator.

Pfizer Building in Brooklyn, New York, circa 1849.

1849: Charles Pfizer & Company opens as a fine-chemicals business. The company produces its first medical breakthrough product, candied santonin — a palatable antiparasitic.

1868: Many of the drugs Union forces used during the Civil War were supplied by Pfizer. In 1868, Pfizer opens new corporate offices at 81 Maiden Lane in Manhattan's Wall Street district to accommodate growth experienced during the war.

1882: Spurred by America's westward expansion, Pfizer opens offices and a warehouse in Chicago, Illinois, its first location outside New York.

1862: First domestic production of tartaric acid and cream of tartar, vital to food and chemical industries, is launched by Pfizer.

1880: Using imported concentrates of lemon and lime, Pfizer begins manufacturing citric acid, which becomes the company's main product and the launching pad of its growth in the years to follow.

1919: The company successfully pioneers the mass production of citric acid by fermentation, an achievement that eventually frees Pfizer from dependency on European citrus growers.

SECTION I

ONE OF AMERICA'S FIRST CHEMICAL companies, Pfizer was founded in Brooklyn in 1849 by Charles Pfizer and Charles Erhart, enterprising young cousins from Germany. Their first product was an antiparasitic called santonin, which they made palatable by blending it with almond-toffee flavoring. Spurred by the success of their innovation, they soon marketed a variety of industrial and medicinal products, several of which had never before been produced in America.

In 1880, Pfizer began manufacturing citric acid from citrus fruit, a product that would propel its growth for many decades. In perfecting the fermentation technology later used to produce citric acid, Pfizer developed a unique expertise which, some 60 years later, enabled it to become the first company to successfully mass-produce penicillin. This remarkable achievement laid the foundation for Pfizer's transformation from a chemical company into a pharmaceutical giant.

1924: Charles Pfizer & Company Inc. turns 75. A celebration at the Brooklyn plant, which has 306 employees, marks the milestone.

1939: Pfizer succeeds so well in the production of citric acid by fermenting molasses that a pound of citric acid, which cost $1.25 in 1919, tumbles to 20¢, and Pfizer is widely recognized as a leader in fermentation technology.

1942: On June 2, Pfizer incorporates in Delaware and on June 22, goes public with an initial offering of 240,000 shares of common stock.

1928: Alexander Fleming discovers the antibiotic properties of the penicillin mold, an event destined to make medical history and to change the course of Pfizer's future.

1941: Pfizer responds to an appeal from the U.S. government to expedite the manufacture of penicillin to treat Allied soldiers fighting in World War II. Of the companies pursuing mass production of penicillin, Pfizer alone uses deep-tank fermentation technology.

1944: Pfizer is successful in its efforts to mass-produce penicillin and becomes the world's largest producer of the "miracle drug." Most of the penicillin that goes ashore with Allied forces on D-Day is made by Pfizer.

Wilhelmine Klotz Erhart; her son, Charles Erhart (seated); and her nephew Charles Pfizer. This photo was taken sometime between 1855 and 1860, after the cousins had founded Charles Pfizer & Company in Brooklyn.

CHAPTER ONE

THE ENTERPRISE BEGINS

1849–1899

In those days, the vast open reaches of North America, laden with promise for the future, exerted an almost magical lure, and those who heard the call most strongly were certainly not the dregs, but more often the cream.

— *The Ludwigsburger Kreiszeitung*

FROM THE VERY BEGINning, innovation, excellence, and a spirit of enterprise characterized Pfizer. Drawn by the seemingly limitless opportunities offered by 19th-century America, the company's founders, Charles Pfizer and Charles Erhart, cousins from Ludwigsburg, Germany, set out to make their mark in the new world.

In 1848, Pfizer, 25, and Erhart, 28, made up their minds. They were willing to risk the dangers of a six-week ocean voyage, motivated by their belief that their ingenuity and expertise in fine chemicals would enable them to prosper and build a thriving enterprise.

The young men had prepared themselves well. Like most sons from well-to-do families of the time, Pfizer and Erhart had both served apprenticeships in trade, the former learning chemistry as an apothecary's apprentice, and the latter learning the grocer's and confectioner's trades from his uncle, Charles Pfizer's father, Karl Frederick Pfizer.

What's more, the cousins' thirst for knowledge was insatiable. At home in Germany, young Pfizer, for example, studied chemistry during the day, taking copious notes of formulas and processes, and then, late at night, devoured all that he could about American history, the English language, and business.

When the young men crossed the Atlantic in 1848, they carried with them a solid grounding in their trades and a vision of what they could achieve, coupled with a willingness to work hard to make that vision a reality.

Trained as a chemist, Charles Pfizer realized that the industrial revolution was bringing science into the workplace. Chemicals that once interested only scholars were becoming indispensable in manufacturing, agriculture, and medicine. He also recognized that in the new nation of America, virtually no one was meeting the growing demand.

What he needed was a stable base of operations and a foothold in the marketplace. When, in 1849, he found both in the village of Williamsburg, a section of Brooklyn, New York, he borrowed $2,500 from his father and bought a modest red brick building on the corner of Bartlett and Tompkins streets. This building became the company's all-purpose center of operations. Serving as an office, laboratory, factory, and warehouse, the

Born in 1684, Johannes Jacob Pfizer, a philosopher and doctor of theology in Ludwigsburg, was Charles Pfizer's paternal great-great-grandfather.

site has remained a vibrant presence throughout Pfizer's history.

The newly formed Charles Pfizer & Company, founded in 1849, aimed to make chemicals not then produced in the United States and immediately set itself apart through its use of innovation, spirit of enterprise, and willingness to take risks to develop scientifically advanced products.

The world of mid–19th century America was a far cry from the world we know today. The streets in New York were lit with whale oil. Stagecoaches circulated in the streets of Brooklyn, and huge, steam-driven paddle wheelers churned up and down the East River.

Life was not only more primitive, it was also filled with dangers. For example, the lack of refrig-

The original $1,000 mortgage, dated October 8, 1850, between Charles Pfizer and Peter A. Delmonico. The first Pfizer plant was located on the property referred to in this document.

eration meant that a diet of meat and potatoes carried the constant risk of intestinal worms. Indeed, these pests caused some of the most common digestive disorders in America. Unfortunately, the taste of the remedy used to treat this condition — santonin, an extract of the Middle Eastern plant Levant wormseed — was so bitter that few people would even swallow it.

Pfizer's First Product

This dilemma was made to order for Pfizer's chemical expertise and Erhart's confectionery skills. Working together, the cousins blended santonin with an almond-toffee flavoring and shaped it into a candy cone that tasted almost like toffee — palatable for the patient, but poison for the parasites.

The "new" santonin was a tremendous success, and soon this innovative remedy was in demand throughout Brooklyn, New York City, and beyond. Buoyed by their success, the cousins began to diversify. By producing relatively small but pure quantities of chemicals not previously manufactured in the United States, they turned tariff laws to their advantage, selling products at lower prices than their foreign competitors.

Within 10 years, raw materials from all over the world were pouring into Charles Pfizer & Company, and more than a dozen chemicals — including borax, camphor, and iodine — were pouring out.

The American economy was booming. The cousins' fledgling enterprise prospered, and they seized every chance to expand their operations. Over the next 30 years, they invested $50,000 to buy 72 lots of land surrounding their Bartlett Street factory. They also opened an office on Beekman Street in Manhattan's drug and chemical district in 1857. Later, they expanded their operations, moving the company's headquarters in 1868 to the Wall Street area, where they bought and remodeled a post–Revolutionary War mansion at 81 Maiden Lane.

As Charles Pfizer & Company grew, its founders' attention to detail never wavered. They maintained close contact with their European suppliers and traveled frequently to Europe on buying trips. On one of them, Charles Erhart proposed to his cousin Fanny Pfizer, Charles Pfizer's sister. When they married in New York in 1856, Erhart and Pfizer became brothers-in-law as well as cousins.

Three years later, Charles Pfizer met and married Anna Hausch on a visit to Germany. His daughter described her parents' first, fateful encounter:

While participating in a local celebration and marching in a parade, "…he was struck dead-on by a bouquet of violets. He looked up and his eyes met those of Anna Hausch. He tried to reach the balcony where she was, but she had already disappeared. Ever a man of action, my father hunted her down, found her that night at a ball, and got himself introduced. They were married shortly thereafter."

The 1860s witnessed the outbreak of the American Civil War, which quickly became one of the most devastating medical events of the 19th century. While the North and South fought each other, the real winner was disease. It took a higher toll than all the bullets that felled many of the 630,000 Americans who died in the war.

Smallpox vaccinations protected soldiers against at least one deadly disease, but there was no defense against a grim assortment of others, including dysentery, malaria, typhoid, yellow fever, and numerous venereal diseases.

Demand for painkillers, preservatives, and disinfectants soared. Eager to stem the suffering, and ever ready to expand, Charles Pfizer & Company moved quickly to fill the void. The company stepped up production of tartaric acid, which was used as a laxative and skin coolant. It also increased production of cream of tartar, which was effective as both a diuretic and a cleansing agent.

With the United States desperate for iodine, which was widely used as a germicide and disinfectant, Pfizer offered to increase production levels and in exchange gained permission to expand its facilities. Since the techniques used to manufacture iodine were similar to those used to produce tartar, Pfizer began producing the iodine immediately in very large quantities. At the same time, the company moved aggressively to develop and ramp up production of other urgently needed drugs, such as morphine, chloroform, and camphor. Purgatives and fungicides, iodine, iodine derivatives, and mercurials were also in great demand. In addition to medicinal applications, mercurials were used in the emerging field of photography, the new medium

Above: Anna Hausch, whom Charles Pfizer met during one of his trips to Ludwigsburg. The two were married in Germany in 1859.

Below: The original caption on this 1861 etching of Manhattan reads, "View of 2nd Ave. looking up from 42nd St." Pfizer's Corporate World Headquarters complex currently stands on the left.

Pfizer established corporate offices at 81 Maiden Lane in 1868 to accommodate the company's growth during the Civil War, when it supplied many drugs used by Northern forces.

Inset: Pfizer made many of the products that found their way into wooden field kits, like this one, used by surgeons during the Civil War.

that Mathew Brady and others would employ to chronicle the war.

The Civil War years were a defining period for the company. The product line grew substantially. Revenues doubled, and the cousins hired 150 new workers. By 1868, the company's sales were surging, and the time had come to open a new office. The new address, 81 Maiden Lane in Manhattan, would become a Pfizer institution for close to a century.

Personal and Professional Success

The Pfizer and Erhart families were also growing. In 1860, Anna Pfizer gave birth to Charles, Jr., followed by Gustave in 1861 and Emile in 1864. Two daughters, Helen and Alice, would later complete the family. In 1863, after living in the United States for nearly two decades, building a successful business, and enjoying the blessings of a healthy and happy family, Charles Pfizer became an American citizen.

Above: The Pfizer family on holiday in Stuttgart, Germany, in 1870. From left: Emile, Charles, Sr., Charles, Jr., Anna, Helen, and Gustave. A second daughter, Alice, was born in 1877.

Above left: The Erhart family, photographed around 1870.

Below: In 1876, the United States celebrated its 100th birthday at the International Centennial Exposition in Philadelphia, and Charles Pfizer & Company won the prestigious Centennial Award (inset).

A few years later, in 1868, the Erharts welcomed their son, William Erhart. Destined for leadership, he would one day become chairman of the board and serve the company until 1940.

In the latter half of the 19th century, the American chemical industry was still in its infancy, but Pfizer was sprinting ahead, delivering products others could not match and offering unassailable leadership in quality.

The cousins' obsession with quality had become legendary. By the 1860s, "Pfizer Quality" had become a recognized catch phrase, and would-be competitors honored the company as the industry's standard-bearer.

The International Centennial Exposition in Philadelphia in 1876, celebrating America's first centennial, thrust Pfizer into the national spotlight. Ten million visitors came to inspect exhibits featuring the latest feats of technology. Pfizer was awarded one of the Exposition's most prestigious honors. It was the only chemical manufacturer to win the Centennial Award for unmatched quality and excellence in its industry.

Pfizer's reputation as a forward-looking company was growing. Its founders enthusiastically embraced

PFIZER PRODUCTS

Cream of Tartar, Tartaric Acid, and Rochelle Salts

These three products were among Pfizer's most popular for decades. Cream of tartar represented a quantum leap for beleaguered late–19th century cooks, who disliked the time-consuming demands of yeast. Cream of tartar was not only quicker, it was also an excellent preserving agent that retarded the spoilage of baked goods. Rochelle salts gained popularity as a mild laxative and as one of the main ingredients in Seidlitz powders, a cathartic. A wine by-product, tartaric acid had a wide variety of uses, including medicinal applications.

Borax

Borax was originally used as a topical antiseptic and a preservative of meat, butter, and other foods. At first, Pfizer manufactured it from imported raw material. Then, in 1864, it was successfully mined in dry lake beds in California, and by 1882, mining operations had begun in Death Valley. From there, borax was hauled 165 miles across parched land to the Mojave railhead by teams of 20 mules that pulled almost 50,000 pounds.

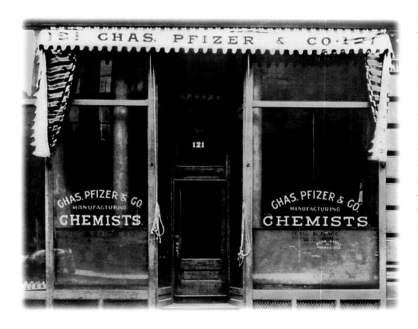

new technologies as well as ideas promoting innovation and efficiency. In 1878, the company bet on the future once again, becoming the first in the industry to use Alexander Graham Bell's new invention, the telephone.

In 1880, Charles Pfizer & Company began manufacturing citric acid, which would fuel Pfizer's explosive growth for years to come. Refined from concentrated fruit juices, citric acid was used for everything from making paper and dissolving iron oxides to flavoring foods and soft drinks, which were becoming the rage nationwide. Pfizer soon became the leading producer of citric acid in the United States.

Pfizer opened this office at 121 Franklin Street in 1892, ten years after it began operations in Chicago, its first site outside New York.

Iodine

Iodine, a widely used germicide and disinfectant in the 19th and early 20th centuries, became one of Pfizer's leading products. The company imported its raw material from Chile, Scotland, and France.

Citric Acid

Extracted from concentrated juices of lemons, limes, and oranges, citric acid initially was used in the processing of pharmaceutical salts such as citrate of magnesia, a popular laxative. However, as sales of carbonated soft drinks took off, demand for citric acid soared. Pfizer began producing this product in 1880, using imported

Opposite page: An 1852 formula book records processes used by Pfizer to produce chemicals.

Above: Advertisements and accounting records from the 1880s.

raw citrus. Realizing that lemons and limes were often available only in limited quantities, the company set out to develop innovative methods to produce citric acid through fermentation.

Camphor

During the latter half of the 19th century, Pfizer's Brooklyn plant became known as the "camphor factory," indicating the product's central role in the company's early success. With its penetrating odor and pungent taste, camphor was prized as a broad-based painkiller and was used as a liniment, an insect repellent, and even a remedy for the common cold.

The rising influence of the camphor factory mirrored the changes in the once-quaint Brooklyn village of Williamsburg, where Pfizer first opened its doors in 1849. By the 1870s, the village had become home to shipbuilding concerns, woodworking businesses, and iron works, and Brooklyn's population swelled to 800,000, making it the fourth largest city in the United States.

Even before the first transcontinental railroad was begun, Pfizer was expanding westward and setting its sights on America's wild frontier. The company already had a large list of clients west of the Mississippi River, and the numbers were quickly increasing. In 1882, Pfizer officially joined America's westward boom, sending John Anderson to open operations in Chicago. Anderson had begun his career at Pfizer in 1873 as a 16-year-old office boy whose primary job was to start the fire every morning in the potbellied stove at 81 Maiden Lane. Years later, he would become president, chair-

man of the board, and one of the company's owners, fueling Pfizer's growth for years to come.

New Generation

As the company's golden anniversary approached, a new generation of leaders was rising through the ranks. Charles Pfizer, Jr., joined the company in 1880, followed by his younger brother Emile in 1887. William Erhart

An 1892 contract for phone service in New York City. Pfizer was the first chemical company to use phone service in the city.

The two contenders for the company's leadership were a study in contrasts. Charles Pfizer, Jr., was enamored of high society and all its trappings. He was much taken, for example, with satin breeches and thoroughbred horses. John Anderson, on the other hand, was a no-nonsense individual whose values had been shaped by his single-minded focus on the business and his unquestioning devotion to the company.

Clearly, the senior Pfizer felt more confident entrusting his company's future to John Anderson's uncompromising values and solid character, and Anderson wasted little time in showing that he was the right choice.

When in 1890 the Japanese government restricted the supplies needed for camphor, a move that could have crippled the company's ability to produce one of its leading products, Anderson responded boldly. In partnership with two other businesses, he formed the Oriental Importing

Oil paintings of Charles Erhart, above, and Charles Pfizer, Sr., circa 1890.

had already been working there for three years when his father, Charles, died on December 27, 1891. The *Brooklyn Daily Eagle* memorialized the cofounder of Pfizer: "Mr. Erhart's sterling qualities, unostentatious charity, and uniform kindness in his daily intercourse with men endeared him to many friends."

Erhart left a partnership worth nearly $250,000 to his son. However, the agreement stipulated that Charles Pfizer could buy William's share at half its inventory value — an option Pfizer quickly exercised, thereby consolidating ownership of the company in his hands.

By then in his 70s, Charles Pfizer was finding it increasingly difficult to manage his growing empire. In 1892, he decided to call John Anderson, his budding superstar, back from Chicago and appoint him general manager of the company.

At the time, Anderson was only 35 years old, and, not surprisingly, his elevation to general managership did not sit well with Pfizer's heir, who had always assumed that he would succeed his father.

John Anderson, who had joined the company in 1873, was the only director in 1900 who was not a Pfizer or an Erhart.

and Manufacturing Company, thereby ensuring an adequate, uninterrupted flow of crude camphor.

By the close of the century, Charles Pfizer & Company had reached the heights of the American chemical business. Starting with only one product, it had built up a portfolio of fine chemicals anchored by camphor, citric acid, cream of tartar, and borax. Other Pfizer products ranged from iodine to strychnine, with a wide array of industrial and pharmacological products in between. The company had offices in New York and Chicago, and its contacts in the import-export business crisscrossed the world.

On December 20, 1899, the Drug Trade Club in New York filled with sounds of celebration as the Pfizer corporate family marked its 50th anniversary. When Charles Pfizer, Sr., walked to the front of the room to speak, the revelers grew still, waiting to hear the words of the entrepreneur who had parlayed a $2,500 loan from his father into one of the country's leading producers of chemical products.

"Our goal," he said, "has been and continues to be the same: to find a way to produce the highest-quality products, and to perfect the most efficient way to accomplish this, in order to best serve our customers. This company has built itself on its reputation and its dedication to these standards, and if we are to celebrate another 50 years, we must always be aware that quality is the keystone."

Quality, innovation, performance, and customer focus had marked Pfizer even as a fledgling enterprise, and they would prove indispensable allies as the company moved into the 20th century and into a more competitive marketplace.

Brooklyn employees gather for a photograph in the yard of Building 6 in 1904.

CHAPTER TWO

A NEW LEADER TAKES COMMAND

My father, having started at the bottom, understood how important morale is to the success of a company. He believed that an employee who feels appreciated will do his best for the company.

— George Anderson, 1948

AT THE TURN OF THE CENTURY, America was really two countries. One was the highly developed East Coast with its boisterous, booming cities. The other, despite Horace Greeley's admonition to go West, was still a vast, hostile wilderness between Chicago and California dotted with a few small, struggling towns.

Charles Pfizer & Company had carved out a strong and growing presence in the East and had made great progress in developing business in the West. The company entered the 20th century with a reputation for unparalleled quality and a successful strategy of controlled expansion into premium chemicals. But great challenges loomed, as Charles Pfizer prepared to retire and the company continued to search for more reliable sources of raw materials.

Closer to home, the opening of the Williamsburg Bridge in Brooklyn on December 21, 1903, was the best Christmas present Charles Pfizer & Company could have received. It provided an immediate boost to business by cutting in half the time wagons needed to reach Manhattan.

The company was also establishing new links with the world. At the start of the 20th century, Pfizer began to take on the first characteristics of a multinational, creating alliances that eventually would stretch from North America around the world. Driving this strategic change was Pfizer's bedrock product, citric acid.

As new drinks like Coca-Cola, Dr Pepper, and Pepsi-Cola gained popularity, Pfizer became a dominant player in the citric acid market. Nevertheless, the company's dependence upon Italian and French growers of lemons and limes left Pfizer at the mercy of its suppliers.

In order to ensure supplies of crude argols for another important Pfizer product, tartars, the company established the Société Anonyme pour le Commerce de Tartre de France in Montpelier, France, in 1905. William Voight, who was named to lead the new venture, was granted power of attorney by the Pfizer board to make purchases of crude argols in France and Algeria.

Pfizer established another major alliance that year when it formed the Chlorine Products Company, which united the skills of Pfizer, the R&H Chemical Company, and the Albany Chemical Company. The new enterprise manufactured chloroform for its parent companies, and in 1906, the Chlorine Products Company leased property to build a facility at Niagara

A bottle of citric acid, Pfizer's most important product at the turn of the century. This citric acid was made from imported raw materials.

Falls, New York, to make chloroform from acetone.

This ambitious enterprise encountered obstacles in 1909, when the Dow Chemical Company, using a new process, started manufacturing a better product more cost-effectively. It was a competitive advantage too large to overcome. Eventually, the Chlorine Products Company suspended operations, and Pfizer contracted to buy chloroform from Dow.

Internally, these relatively quiet business years were among the most important in Pfizer's history. In 1892, the senior Pfizer welcomed Charles, his 32-year-old son and namesake, into the company as a partner and owner. A few years later, in 1900, the company filed an official certificate of incorporation in the state of New Jersey, with authorized capital of $2 million, divided into 20,000 shares of $100 each.

Top center: The crest adorning the chimney of Charles Pfizer, Jr.'s, magnificent Bernardsville, New Jersey, home, Yademos. The 18-room Yademos ("someday" spelled backward) was situated on 48 acres that included a swimming pool, tennis court, and seven-room caretaker's cottage.

Above: Alice Pfizer married Baron Bachofen von Echt of Austria. Her sister, Helen, married a British peer, Sir Oliver Duncan. Both women spent most of their lives in Europe.

Right: Emile Pfizer, around 1910, five years after he replaced his brother Charles as company president. Emile ran the company until 1940.

John Anderson in Control

The first board of directors, formed that same year, included Charles Pfizer, Jr., his brother Emile, and William Erhart. Emile and William each received 333 shares of stock, while Charles Pfizer, Jr., had a controlling interest with 334 shares. Although John Anderson was general manager at the time, he had no shares.

By 1900, the rivalry between John Anderson and Charles Pfizer, Jr., had deepened. At the opening board meeting held on May 21, 1900, Charles Pfizer, Jr., took the first of many missteps that would tip the balance of power in favor of his rival. As a token of recognition, the Pfizer heir transferred a single share of stock to John Anderson, giving him the right to a seat on the board. With that, Anderson became the only director not related to the Erhart or Pfizer families.

That single share of stock, however, did not begin to represent the power that John Anderson would eventually wield. Using his value to the company as leverage, Anderson insisted in 1901 upon a five-year agreement to receive 25 percent of the company's net profits, the same amount earned by Charles, Jr., and each of the other stockholders.

Although an established company with strong sales, Pfizer could hardly sustain its president's penchant for disastrous real estate transactions. It is estimated that between 1900 and 1912, Charles Pfizer, Jr., lost more than $2 million on such ventures. These debacles further heightened the tension between him and Anderson.

In December 1905, a special meeting of the board of directors witnessed a corporate duel between Charles Pfizer, Jr., and John Anderson that would leave only one standing. Charles, Jr., was forced to resign. Following his departure, John Anderson, then 48 years old, reorganized the company, assuming the titles of senior director, treasurer, and chairman of the executive committee.

John Anderson did not seek to become president. The right to hold that position remained in the Pfizer family until 1941. Emile Pfizer replaced his brother Charles as president, and Erhart remained vice president. Neither of the cofounders' remaining children attempted to dominate the executive committee during these tumultuous times, presumably out of consideration for the company's best interests.

By the early 1900s, Charles Pfizer, Sr., had suffered the heartbreak of seeing his oldest son driven from the business and dishonored by debt. In 1906, at the age of 82, while vacationing at his Newport, Rhode Island, estate, the elder Pfizer fell down a flight of stairs and suffered severe internal injuries. Complications set in that led to pneumonia. With his daughters, Alice and Helen, at his bedside, Charles Pfizer died on October 19, 1906.

In an October 21, 1906, obituary hailing Pfizer as "one of the best chemists in America," *The New York Tribune* reported that by "bringing to his task a thorough German technical education, great industry, and determination, he successfully met all difficulties and each year expanded his business."

Indeed he did. Charles Pfizer had challenged and extended the horizons of his time. Combining scientific knowledge and innovative ideas with a tireless and optimistic spirit, he tackled some of the hardships of life in the 19th century and made life better for countless patients.

Of all the momentous decisions Charles Pfizer made, placing the company in the hands

Above: Charles Pfizer, Sr., died on October 19, 1906, at the age of 82.

Below: A recent photograph of the home Charles Pfizer, Jr., built in the late 1800s in Bernardsville, New Jersey.

Charles Pfizer, Jr., leaning on the newel post above, and his wife, Nana, seated at center, joined other members of the Essex Hunt for a group photo around 1900. At left, an article describing the hunt.

of John Anderson was perhaps the most far-sighted. The elder Pfizer had had the vision to create and build a great company. John Anderson brought the practical wisdom and concern for his employees that would carry the enterprise forward.

Anderson's first year as head of the company — 1906 — was also the first to report an official record of the company's sales and earnings. Sales stood at $3.4 million, with a net profit of $405,000.

Understanding that morale is as important as money in building a successful business, Anderson won approval that same year for Pfizer's first bonus plan to reward employees for their loyalty and hard work.

During the next four years, Anderson consolidated power. As chairman of the executive committee and a company director, he became Charles Pfizer & Company's undisputed leader. Despite his influence, however, he still owned only a single share of stock. When the contract that entitled him to 25 percent of the company's profits expired on December 31, 1909, John Anderson was in a position to expand his influence.

At the board meeting on February 9, 1910, he quietly, but very firmly, insisted on a stock redistribution. The corporation purchased 83 shares of stock from each of the Pfizers, Emile and Charles, Jr., and William Erhart, at $280 per share, plus one additional share from Charles for $1,200. Anderson then purchased these combined shares for $70,000. This agreement left each director with 250 shares — a quarter of the company — thereby giving Anderson parity with the other three directors, Charles and Emile Pfizer and William Erhart.

With the company's sales totaling nearly $3 million in 1910, Anderson's purchase of a quarter interest in Pfizer for $70,000 was a shrewd bargain. After concluding these successful negotiations, Anderson, for the first time in his life, felt a profound need for a respite. He requested and received a year's leave of absence at full pay with expenses included. He and his son, George, then left for an extended visit to California.

In 1910, Anderson returned to find the company reeling from skyrocketing costs, which by 1911 had wiped out Pfizer's profits and led to its first and only loss — $4,000 in 1911 — since its incorporation.

The rising costs of imported raw materials — particularly tartrates — and the decline in supplies of citrates from Italy were two of the causes. Another was rising competition from foreign manufacturers following passage of the Payne Tariff Act of 1909. Once lower tariffs permitted foreign companies to sell finished products in the United States, demand for raw materials on the European continent soared, exacerbating the run-up in Pfizer's costs and the reduction in its profits.

In 1912, the return of bumper crops and excellent citrus harvests eased the scramble for raw materials. By 1914, Pfizer was profitable again, earning nearly $240,000, and Anderson could point to a tripling of sales in the nine years since he had assumed control.

The pace of change was beginning to quicken around the world. Industrialization, new technologies, modern transportation systems, and medical advances were all opening up a new world of opportunity. Like his mentors, Charles Pfizer, Sr., and Charles Erhart, John Anderson took full advantage of it. But even he could not foresee what monumental challenges lay ahead as war threatened the prosperity that he and his predecessors had worked so hard to achieve.

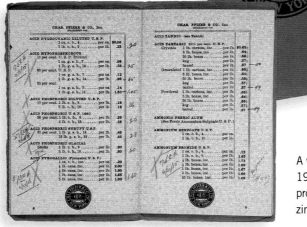

A wholesale price list, circa 1905, lists a broad range of products, from boric acid to zinc sulphocarbolate.

Listeners are urged to buy war bonds during a World War I rally at Pfizer's Brooklyn plant.

CHAPTER THREE

THE WAR YEARS

1914–1919

During our first meeting, Mr. Anderson introduced me to another Pfizer official with the remark, "Dr. Currie is up here now and I think he has something interesting."

— James Currie, 1917

ON JANUARY 29, 1914, THE board of directors created the position of chairman and promptly filled it with John Anderson, the most logical choice. After 41 years of service, Anderson set the board's agenda, although Emile Pfizer and William Erhart continued as president and vice president, respectively. Anderson's son, George, who had also worked for the company for years, joined the board at that same meeting.

John Anderson's most urgent priority was to reduce Pfizer's vulnerability as an importer of raw materials. He recommended establishing two committees that would report to the board of directors at each meeting: a General Committee of four members to supervise the purchase of raw materials and sales of manufactured products, and a Works Committee of three directors to oversee manufacturing and research operations. At the same time, Anderson and Emile Pfizer instructed their buyers to secure as much crude tartar and citrate as they possibly could.

Anderson was moving fast, but not fast enough to outrun developments that would plunge first Europe and then America into what would later become known as the Great War. Storm clouds had been darkening over Europe, and the assassination of Archduke Franz Ferdinand of Austria

in June of 1914 triggered the eruption of hostilities. One by one, nations were drawn into the conflict, which pitted the Central Powers of Germany and Austria-Hungary against the Allied Powers of Great Britain, France, Russia, and eventually, the United States.

Within six months, naval blockades and a cartel of Italian citrus growers put a stranglehold on Pfizer's most important raw materials. Meanwhile, the German submarine blockade held 800 tons of crude tartars hostage in France.

Prices of chemicals and medicinals continued to rise sharply. Delivery of supplies was further blocked, and Pfizer's future was threatened. These problems were compounded when many of Pfizer's best men were drafted into the U.S. Army. Those who served in the military left with John Anderson's personal assurance that they could reclaim their jobs when they returned and that their families would continue to receive paychecks for the duration of the war. Anderson's reassurance demonstrated Pfizer's long-standing tradition of commitment to its people and their welfare.

To support the U.S. war effort, Pfizer gave employees Christmas bonuses in the form of Liberty Bonds, promoted by posters like this one. *(Photo courtesy of Corbis.)*

A Bold Step

Desperate to replenish their vanishing sources of raw materials, Pfizer scientists began working around the clock. This unparalleled effort helped to make Pfizer a leader in fermentation technology, an expertise that would prove critical to the company's success. It took 10 years, but by 1924, Pfizer scientists had perfected the mass production of citric acid from sugar through fermentation.

The process was pioneered by James Currie, a brilliant scientist and former chemist at the U.S. Department of Agriculture who had joined Pfizer in 1917 at the age of 34. He arrived with an audacious idea: to produce citric acid without using citrus. As a government food chemist, Currie had studied fermentation in cheesemaking and discovered that one of the by-products was citric acid. He began a series of fermentation experiments using sugar and bread mold and succeeded in producing small amounts of crude citric acid. Although Currie realized that the results of his experiment could have commercial potential, he also recognized that manufacturing industrial quantities would be an enormous challenge.

Interviewed years later, the man who would be revered as a giant in the history of the chemical industry explained why he had decided to bring his discovery to Pfizer:

I was confident that my work had commercial potentialities in the production of citric acid. In this era, Pfizer, as well as another company in Philadelphia, was a major producer of the product. I decided to go to Pfizer because it was the larger of the two companies, and I entered into correspondence with the company. I met with John Anderson, who was Pfizer's chairman of the board. During our first meeting, Mr. Anderson introduced me to another Pfizer official with the remark, "Dr. Currie is up here now and I think he has something interesting."

"Something interesting" was the tantalizing prospect of producing thousands of tons of citric acid, not from costly imported lemons and limes but from cheap, plentiful, and accessible sugar harvested close to home.

The key was mastering the fermentation process. The stakes were enormous. Success would liberate Pfizer from the tyranny of foreign suppliers and set the stage for the company to dominate the market for the popular chemical. With security an overriding concern, a citric acid committee was formed, and all employees participating in the project signed confidentiality agreements.

In 1919, Currie was joined in his lab by a 16-year-old assistant, Jasper Kane. Working in complete secrecy behind locked doors with all

Above: Chemist James Currie, shown here in later years, joined Pfizer in 1917. He pioneered the production of citric acid by mold fermentation of sugar. This innovation eventually freed Pfizer from its dependence on European citrus growers.

Right: Jasper Kane joined Pfizer in 1919 as James Currie's assistant. Later, as head of the Fermentation Department, he found a way to produce citric acid using molasses, a by-product of sugar manufacture, instead of refined white sugar, thus cutting costs significantly.

documentation placed in a safe, the two began their quest to turn sugar and mold into citric "gold."

Initial results were encouraging. Currie was able to produce citric acid in flasks with a 50 percent yield. But could he take the next step and mass-produce the lab results? The Citric Acid Committee met and developed a plan to produce 100 pounds of citric acid per day.

The production runs met the targets for quantity, but the quality was disappointing. Batch after batch was contaminated by variations in the fermentation medium or by the presence or absence of trace metals, or they went awry as a result of environmental factors such as temperature, humidity, and oxygen.

Right: John L. Smith returned to Pfizer as the plant superintendent in 1919. A fair, hard-driving man, Smith hated waste and often asked employees to show him worn pencil stubs before ordering new pencils.

Below: From flask to pan, and eventually to vat, Currie fought an uphill battle with fermentation. He created the world's first large-scale citric acid fermentation plant at the Brooklyn Works.

John L. Smith

Currie refused to be defeated or dejected. He continued to forge ahead, experimenting in uncharted territory, learning as he went. Two years after he joined Pfizer, Currie received invaluable help with his research in the person of John L. Smith.

Smith had joined the company as a laboratory consultant in 1906, then left in 1914 to work for E.R. Squibb & Sons. He returned to Pfizer in 1919 as plant superintendent. Easily recognizable by his broad shoulders and lantern jaw, Smith was driven, impatient, innovative, ingenious, and exacting, but he was also fair. To communicate more effectively and better monitor the work of his staff, he established a tradition of elegant lunches in the dining room above Warehouse A in Brooklyn. Before sitting down to huge portions of roast

In 1916, John L. Smith, right, enjoys a friendly potato-sack race with fellow Pfizerites. Also pictured are T. Cochrane, left, and A.A. Cheirl.

beef and chicken, each man had to find his seating assignment, designated by a personal napkin ring engraved with his number.

Finding one's number across from Smith was not a good omen. Although Smith metaphorically "ate employees for breakfast," real dressings down invariably occurred at lunch. A crusader against wastefulness, Smith also scrutinized every financial request and asked that his employees show him worn pencil stubs before ordering new pencils.

John Smith injected discipline and harnessed the talents of his team to the fullest. He created the conditions for James Currie and Jasper Kane to develop Pfizer's expertise in deep-tank fermentation and steadily scale up their production of citric acid.

Success in the attempt to produce citric acid through fermentation was not yet in view when suddenly another competitor challenged Pfizer for a share of the market. The Italian cartel Camera Argumaria, which had supplied citrate of lime to the company before World War I, raised export prices on citrate of lime and began extracting citric acid on its own.

John Anderson sprang into action. He bought concentrated lime juice everywhere he could, making purchases from England, the West Indies, and California. New shipments began to arrive, but supplies remained modest and unreliable,

and back orders at the Brooklyn Works continued to grow.

Pfizer's resourcefulness would be tested even further when Prohibition began in 1920, causing the demand for soft drinks made with citric acid to skyrocket.

As John Smith completed his first year as works superintendent, he urged his employees to raise their sights and keep their spirits high. In a tradition that would endure for decades, he initiated the annual letter written to Pfizer employees. The last page was reserved for a personal note describing their contribution to the company. The first annual letter was distributed in 1919, along with a "Christmas compensation" amounting to 10 percent of each employee's yearly salary.

In his first personal note, Smith wrote:

We should make our organization one which is second to none in its initiative and efficiency, and one which is ever on the alert to take advantage of every opportunity to advance the welfare and standing of Charles Pfizer & Company as the preeminent leader in our line. We should set as our standard "the best products in the world manufactured at a cost to compete anywhere."

After World War I ended, Pfizer was forced to scramble for supplies of raw materials to produce tartaric acid.

In 1924, Pfizer celebrated 75 years at its Brooklyn Works location. In a speech, John L. Smith predicted that the SUCIAC process, which was still under development, would finally free Pfizer from dependence on foreign suppliers.

CHAPTER FOUR

'SUCIAC' SPELLS SUCCESS

1920–1930

If our costs are high, we must bring them down; if they are low, make them lower; if the quality is below standard, bring it up to standard; if the quality is good, make it better.

— John L. Smith, 1920

WORKS AND LABORATORIES BOROUGH OF BROOKLYN, NEW YORK

THE 1920s DIDN'T GET off to a roaring start for Charles Pfizer & Company. In the aftermath of World War I, the American economy fell into recession, and unemployment shot up from a little more than 2 percent to nearly 12 percent. American industry had been geared for war, and the sudden end of the conflict left warehouses overstocked and factories tooled for the wrong kind of production.

Despite difficulties in procuring the raw materials to produce citric acid, Pfizer had prospered during the war. Booming demand for its medicines and other core products had ensured the company's success. By 1920, however, sales had declined by 6 percent. The following year, they dropped 52 percent lower.

John Anderson and the Pfizer board concluded that drastic remedies were necessary. They suspended the manufacture of mercury, iodine, and tartar emetic. They also scaled back production of citric acid, tartaric acid, and cream of tartar by 50 percent. In addition, to avoid wholesale layoffs they reduced all salaries and wages by 20 percent, while dedicating the sixth work day to maintenance and repair rather than production.

The postwar recession was severe but short-lived. Nonetheless, the decline resulted in waves of consolidation that produced major changes in the chemical industry. A postwar glut of raw materials, as well as excess plant capacity, led to an explosion in productivity. American companies received another boost when the Treaty of Versailles, which followed the war's end in 1918, sanctioned the forfeiture of German patents, trademarks, and property. A year later, these reparations led to the creation of the Chemical Foundation to administer the patents.

As the industry rose and fell with the economy, James Currie and Jasper Kane remained committed to their work on fermentation. Although confident of their basic approach, they were mired in technical obstacles. Citric acid was unstable, and the vats frequently became contaminated. Transforming sugar into acid citric — Sugar Under Conversion Into Acid Citric (SUCIAC) — was discouragingly slow. Of the 2.9 million pounds of citric acid that Pfizer produced in 1920, SUCIAC fermentation accounted for only 885 pounds.

That same year, John Anderson dispatched his son, George, to Europe on a mission to secure argols, tartars, and other raw materials.

The company's Brooklyn plant appeared on stationery and business cards throughout the 1920s and 1930s.

He returned with alarming news: A new citric acid plant in Palermo, Italy, had the capacity to produce four million pounds of citric acid from citrus fruit annually, and the Italians were gearing up not only to produce but also to sell their own finished product.

The Yields Rise

Currie did not lose heart. Believing that innovation inevitably entails a series of failures that eventually results in success, he adopted another approach. Using Gordon Dryer machines, which controlled humidity and temperature, he experimented with different-sized pans, depths, and temperatures. By the fall of 1921, he had achieved a breakthrough, and yields began to rise. Within months, results had improved so dramatically that John Smith proposed building a plant at the Brooklyn Works devoted solely to the fermentation of citric acid.

By 1922, Currie had achieved yields that were consistently more than 50 percent. Smaller pans, a new ventilation system that forced air down over the pans, and constant fine-tuning all contributed to Pfizer's success. Basing its estimates on the

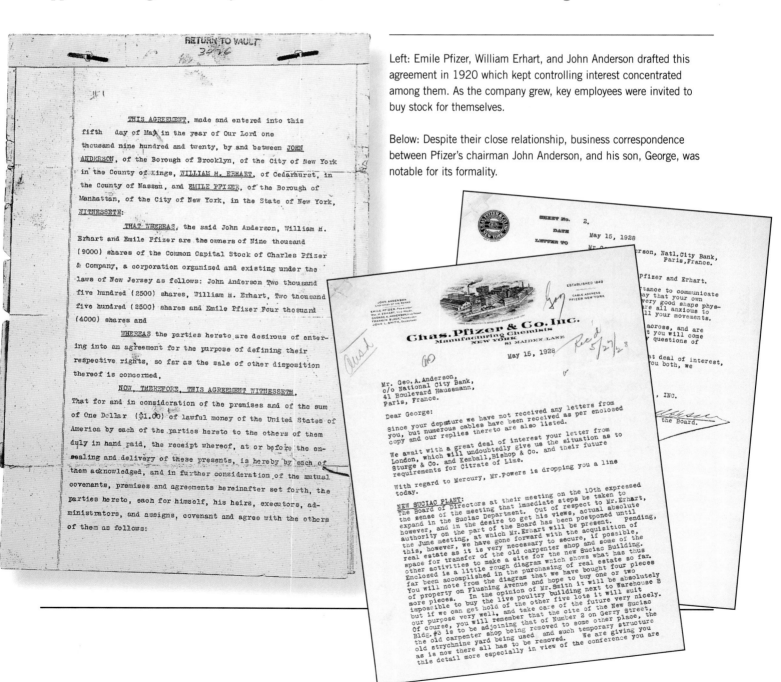

Left: Emile Pfizer, William Erhart, and John Anderson drafted this agreement in 1920 which kept controlling interest concentrated among them. As the company grew, key employees were invited to buy stock for themselves.

Below: Despite their close relationship, business correspondence between Pfizer's chairman John Anderson, and his son, George, was notable for its formality.

results that Currie had achieved, the Citric Acid Committee estimated that a plant running at 50 percent yields could produce as much as 100,000 pounds of citric acid per month.

Convinced that it had overcome major obstacles, the company took a historic, strategic gamble. In December 1922, it decided to close down its borax operation in Building 3B and build a SUCIAC plant in its place. Although Pfizer produced and sold millions of pounds of borax in 1922, the product's use as a food preservative was declining, and the company still lacked control over the raw materials necessary to produce it.

Pfizer continually found itself in a pitched battle for the supplies needed to produce many of its products — from citric, boric, and tartaric acids to camphor and chloroform. This ongoing problem was illustrated by the challenges Pfizer encountered in producing tartaric acid in the early 1920s. Prices had reached a wartime peak of 90 cents per pound, but by 1922, they had plunged to 20 cents. Germany and Italy flooded the U.S. market with tartaric acid, while Pfizer still lacked access to the raw materials needed to match European prices, even through its French subsidiary, the Compagnie de Tartres. Emile Pfizer replaced the subsidiary with the Société Anonyme Produits Tartriques du Midi (PTM), but the new company fared no better than its predecessor.

Meanwhile, in the United States, John Anderson was preparing to celebrate a half century of employment at Pfizer, the only company for which he had ever worked. On July 23, 1923, Anderson joined fellow employees at the Union Club for a celebratory dinner at which he was presented with a gold matchbox. It was a fitting gift for a man who had begun his career at Pfizer lighting stove fires to heat the offices on Maiden Lane.

At a time when most men would have been slowing down, Anderson, then 66, was hitting his

stride. His lifetime of service to Charles Pfizer & Company had earned him enormous respect, both inside the company and throughout the chemical industry. Though a demanding boss, John Anderson earned the loyalty and affection of his employees.

In 1924, the company turned 75 and set its sights on increasing SUCIAC production. John Smith wrote in his annual letter to employees, "We have no problem in this plant to contend with that is more important than the development of the SUCIAC process." Although Pfizer management could have applied for a patent on this process, it decided to keep the process under lock and key. In 1929, an article published in London in the *Chemical Trade Journal & Chemical Engineer* noted that "The American output of natural citric acid is supple-

John Anderson's handwritten negotiations are preserved for history. At the age of 66, he celebrated his 50th anniversary with the company.

mented by acid produced by the mold fermentation of sugar. This process is carried out on a large scale, but production figures have never been published, nor have any but the mere outlines of this process been [described]."

In five short years, Smith had almost completely transformed the Chemical Department, introducing a greater emphasis on new scientific principles and bringing a strong, fresh stimulus to Pfizer research and development. His first thrust was to provide the energy and direction that brought to a culmination the research program in citric acid.

Smith was personally on hand for the start-up of any operation and kept a constant eye on any new construction in progress. He worked long hours, including nights and Saturdays, was acquainted with all the details of the operations and was a thoroughly competent scientist.

Building 21

Under Smith's guidance, the SUCIAC process continued to show promise, and he believed it had

the potential to change the entire face of the citric acid industry. Innovations like the one that grew out of the SUCIAC project marked Pfizer as a leader in the industry and positioned the company for the tremendous growth that it would experience as Pfizer headed into its next 75 years. After the first full year, the SUCIAC plant produced almost one million pounds of citric acid, slightly more than a third of the 2.9 million pounds made using the conventional extraction method. Recognizing SUCIAC's potential, Smith proposed to the board of directors in 1925 that the company build a new plant dedicated to the production of citric acid.

Building 21, a seven-story structure that was completed in nine months, began operating on New Year's Day of 1926, a monument to Pfizer's self-reliance.

Pfizer's increased capacity fortified SUCIAC's presence in the citric acid market. Since 1915, the

Early attempts at fermentation included experiments in which shakers were used to aerate flasks of broth.

price of citric acid had dropped from 41 to 15.5 cents per pound. With Pfizer prepared to outflank the Italian monopoly and establish firm control over the market, the days of citrus derivatives were clearly numbered. By 1926, production of citric acid using the new fermentation techniques had decisively outdistanced those that relied on lemons and limes

Within two years, Pfizer dominated citric acid production. When the Italian-based Camera cartel abruptly shut off its export supply of citrate of lime, reserving it for Italian production of citric acid, the California citrus industry easily filled the gap.

Pfizer delivery trucks were an increasingly common sight on the streets of New York City as the company steadily expanded.

In 1928, the Pfizer executive committee approved further expansion of the SUCIAC project, dedicating nearly $1 million for a second SUCIAC building (called 21A). In response to the Italian embargo, Pfizer also began supplying the English firm Kemball-Bishop with citrate of lime. Pfizer's alliance with Kemball-Bishop prefigured the many strategic partnerships that would characterize Pfizer in the latter part of the 20th century.

Building 21 had been hailed as a technical marvel, but Building 21A was nothing short of revolutionary. Since Pfizer was far ahead of its competition, all the equipment for the building had to be custom manufactured to exact specifications. The new plant opened its doors in July 1929, and from that date, fermentation moved steadily from shallow pans to deep vats.

Pfizer reached another milestone that same year. For the first time, it used no lemon juice, lime juice, or foreign citrate of lime to manufacture its citric acid. The result was 14 million pounds of citric acid produced as SUCIAC liquor, then refined into 5.9 million pounds of citric acid, 10.3 million pounds of citrate of lime, and 900,000 pounds of sodium citrate.

Not content to rest on his laurels, Jasper Kane began working with his colleague Alexander Finlay to perfect deep-tank fermentation. As they searched for a way to provide more air to the process, they discovered a method that would enable them to bubble sterile air through the liquor and blend it using electrical mixers. If perfected, the process would eliminate the danger of contamination.

Although still in the developmental stage, the project would have major consequences for Pfizer and the world: The company's mastery of deep-tank fermentation technology would hold the key to one of the greatest medical breakthroughs of all time — the mass production of penicillin.

In the meantime, Pfizer searched for new applications for its expertise in fermentation. Under Currie's guidance, the Research Department began looking for ways to use fermentation to produce other chemicals, including gluconic, salicylic, tartaric, and succinic acids.

Pfizer also worked to develop its own source of raw materials for tartaric acid. In the summer of 1928, Smith recommended that John McKeen supervise the attempt to produce tartrate of lime, the first step in making tartaric acid from low-grade acid tartars. Producing crude tartaric acid in the Brooklyn Works would double the company's capacity without additional investment.

In his annual letter for 1929, John Smith explained the rationale for Pfizer's search for new products and processes: "It is the Company's purpose to make a very serious effort to add to our line of new products, which have potential possibilities as to their commercial applications in large volumes."

Another important development came on January 10, 1929, when John Anderson announced that he was stepping down as chairman of the

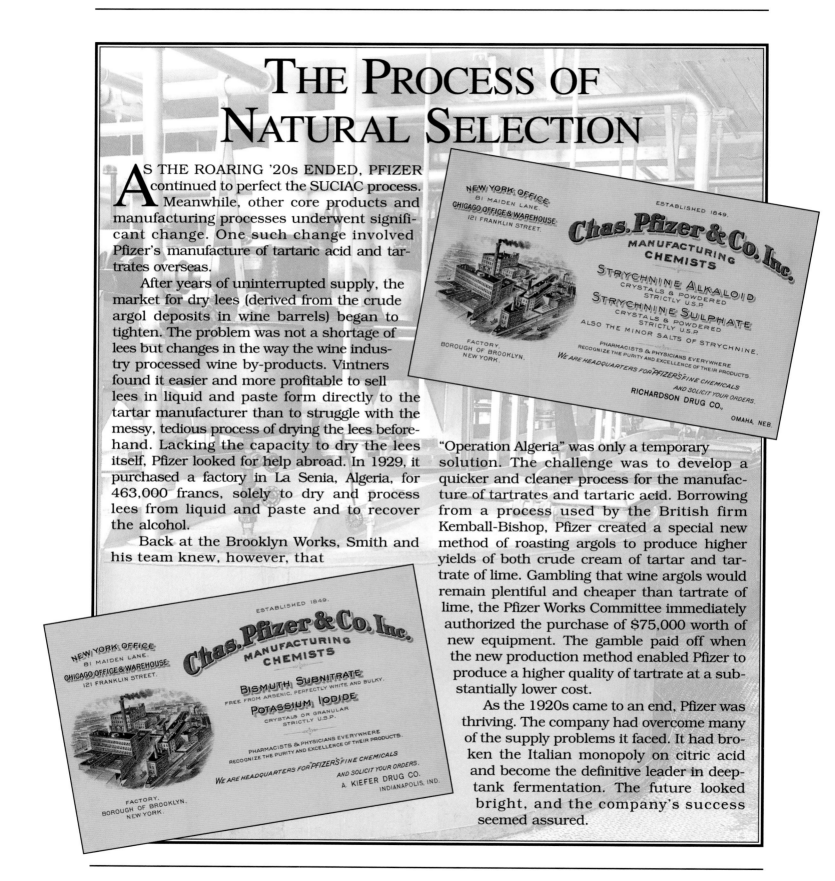

THE PROCESS OF NATURAL SELECTION

AS THE ROARING '20s ENDED, PFIZER continued to perfect the SUCIAC process. Meanwhile, other core products and manufacturing processes underwent significant change. One such change involved Pfizer's manufacture of tartaric acid and tartrates overseas.

After years of uninterrupted supply, the market for dry lees (derived from the crude argol deposits in wine barrels) began to tighten. The problem was not a shortage of lees but changes in the way the wine industry processed wine by-products. Vintners found it easier and more profitable to sell lees in liquid and paste form directly to the tartar manufacturer than to struggle with the messy, tedious process of drying the lees beforehand. Lacking the capacity to dry the lees itself, Pfizer looked for help abroad. In 1929, it purchased a factory in La Senia, Algeria, for 463,000 francs, solely to dry and process lees from liquid and paste and to recover the alcohol.

Back at the Brooklyn Works, Smith and his team knew, however, that

"Operation Algeria" was only a temporary solution. The challenge was to develop a quicker and cleaner process for the manufacture of tartrates and tartaric acid. Borrowing from a process used by the British firm Kemball-Bishop, Pfizer created a special new method of roasting argols to produce higher yields of both crude cream of tartar and tartrate of lime. Gambling that wine argols would remain plentiful and cheaper than tartrate of lime, the Pfizer Works Committee immediately authorized the purchase of $75,000 worth of new equipment. The gamble paid off when the new production method enabled Pfizer to produce a higher quality of tartrate at a substantially lower cost.

As the 1920s came to an end, Pfizer was thriving. The company had overcome many of the supply problems it faced. It had broken the Italian monopoly on citric acid and become the definitive leader in deep-tank fermentation. The future looked bright, and the company's success seemed assured.

The Joint Meeting of the Sales and Scientific Staffs of Chas. Pfizer and Co. Inc.

board, bringing to a close three decades of dedicated service and inspired leadership. Anderson left an unmatched legacy of loyalty to and love of his company. He remained on the executive committee, but within a year, Pfizer's new leadership had fallen into place. William Erhart became the new chairman, Emile Pfizer assumed the presidency, and George, Anderson's son, rose to senior vice president.

As the 1920s drew to a close, Pfizer celebrated a successful decade with the first meeting of its sales and scientific staff in December 1929. The meeting, which became a biannual tradition, was intended to keep the sales staff abreast of new

In December 1929, Pfizer held its first science and sales meeting. The meeting, which took place in New York, brought the scientific and sales staffs closer together. The group in the right foreground includes John L. Smith, second from left; William Erhart, with hands resting on chair; John Anderson, with hands clasped; and John Powers, Sr., behind Anderson.

Pfizer products. The highlight of the December meeting was a festive gathering at Sherry's restaurant in Manhattan, captured for posterity in a historic photograph.

The Brooklyn plant's administration building, circa 1941. Today, it is home to an innovative Pfizer-supported school called Beginning with Children.

CHAPTER FIVE

THE DEPRESSION YEARS

1930–1939

Business conditions are poor at the present time, and unless the company can achieve that superiority for which it is striving and for which it is paying, it must give serious consideration to a reduction of our staff, comparable to the degree of efficiency now prevailing.

— John L. Smith, 1932

ON OCTOBER 24, 1929, A WAVE of panic hit brokers, investors, and Wall Street bankers as the stock market plummeted to unprecedented lows. "Black Thursday" was an erupting volcano that would eventually bury most of corporate America in the ashes of financial ruin. The chemical industry found itself mainly out of range of the disaster, although not entirely immune.

From 1931 to 1939, the industry grew from $2.6 billion to $3.7 billion, seeming to substantiate *Chemical Week*'s assertion that the chemical business was "depression proof." As the publication pointed out, the industry "had so many customers, ranging from … individual[s] … to almost every industry imaginable," that it was somewhat insulated from economic ups and downs. The resultant growth of the chemical business enabled the industry to invest heavily in research throughout the 1920s, with momentum picking up even more in the 1930s.

This research resulted in a host of new products, and the 1930s became the decade of vitamins, hormones, and sulfa drugs. Neither the industry nor Pfizer, however, could entirely escape the economic deluge that had engulfed so many other businesses. The company's revenues and earnings fell during the first years of the Great Depression. President Hoover continued to express confidence that prosperity was just around the corner, but

John Smith's predictions proved more accurate than those of the president. In his annual letter, Smith warned employees to prepare for an extended downturn:

There is ample evidence everywhere of the severity of the present depression, and we believe that every important man of our organization is sufficiently alive to the acuteness of the situation to make comment in this direction unnecessary.

The obligation is imposed upon each department head and assistant to reduce production costs and at the same time not only maintain, but further improve the quality of our products. This involves precise supervision and the study of each process by the respective department head to bring about economies and betterment of quality.

Smith emphasized that "it is the company's policy not to reduce salaries or wages," but warned that conditions could become dire enough to require such measures.

Discord flared when Pfizer's Ways and Means Committee recommended the forced retirement of two older men in the Sales Department as a way to

This logo has adorned the Brooklyn administration building for decades.

save salaries and to motivate younger salesmen to produce more. John Anderson, then 73, chided the committee for suggesting that loyal men be required to retire:

> *Has the effect of the recommendations of the Ways and Means Committee been properly considered by all? You seem to think that it will be stimulating on the others of the sales force — but it may be very disheartening and cause others of our men to feel that after spending the flower of their life with us … they will be thrown out, on five minutes notice, like old lumber.*

The Great Depression continued to deepen. By 1932, 16 million Americans — one quarter of the working population — were out of work. In 1931, Pfizer sales plunged 27 percent and net income fell 58 percent. Smith froze hiring, suspended raises, and eliminated overtime.

THE VITAMIN LEADER

THE TERM "VITAMIN" WAS FIRST COINED in 1912 by Casimir Funk, the discoverer of vitamin B. Over the next 20 years, research indicated that vitamins enhanced nutrition, and in 1919, British scientists demonstrated that improved nutrition could heal children with scurvy and rickets.

When continuing research proved that other diseases were also linked to a lack of vitamins, the race was on to produce them commercially.

Pfizer's expertise in fermentation technology gave it an advantage in vitamin research and production. Led by Drs. Richard Pasternack and Gordon Cragwell, Pfizer isolated vitamin C, or ascorbic acid, from cabbage. At the time, researchers at the University of Basel in Switzerland and at Abbott Laboratories had developed a method that employed the fermentation of sorbose. Obtaining licenses for both processes, Pfizer started production of ascorbic acid in 1935.

By 1936, Pfizer could exhibit a large vat of its manmade vitamin C at the Chemical Show, while Merck and Roche had produced only minuscule samples. Pasternack developed a fermentation-free production method, and after building a new plant and initiating a 24-hour-a-day, seven-day-a-week production schedule, Pfizer became the world's leading producer of vitamin C.

One of the company's first customers was the Soviet Union, which purchased the product under the Lend-Lease Act of 1941. Demand also rose rapidly across America as more positive applications were found, including use as a food preservative, a fruit-enhancing agent, and a dietary supplement.

Encouraged by its success with vitamin C, Pfizer pushed ahead in 1938 with production of vitamin B-2, or riboflavin. After scientists discovered that milling and bleaching common flour eliminated most of its nutrients, the government began recommending that not only flour but also a large array of other foods be enriched with vitamin B-2. Jasper Kane and a Pfizer team developed a vitamin mix that included riboflavin, thiamin, niacin, and iron.

Following World War II, Pfizer further expanded its vitamin research, successfully isolating and concentrating vitamin B-12 in a fermentation process. From vitamin B-12, the company moved on to vitamin A, and by the late 1940s, Pfizer had become the established leader in the manufacture of vitamins.

Richard Pasternack's fermentation-free production method enabled Pfizer to become the world's leading producer of vitamin C.

How much longer could Pfizer avoid layoffs? With the exception of the SUCIAC and Cream of Tartar departments, most of the company was already working a four-day week. John Smith mandated that "department heads should rotate the employees so that, in the aggregate, there will be reduction in the number of working hours."

Even with cost reductions, there was simply not enough work. Layoffs loomed on the horizon. Emile Pfizer dreaded losing good workers, and he knew that when conditions improved, Pfizer would need those people back. In 1932, he donated $250,000 of his own money to keep workers employed at least three days a week. Asked what the workers would do, he responded, "They can paint and clean." Remarkably, no one was laid off, although salaries were cut by 10 percent in June of 1932.

Emile Pfizer's donation of a quarter of a million dollars was a fortune in the 1930s, but in the decades to come, his employees repaid it many times over with their heartfelt loyalty and gratitude.

As Pfizer struggled through the economic storm, it forged ahead in basic research. In 1933, the company achieved an enormous breakthrough in citric acid, its most important product. Jasper Kane discovered a way to use molasses, a by-product of sugar manufacture, to replace more expensive cane sugar. Within a year, Pfizer was producing 5.9 million pounds of citric acid, of which 5.8 million pounds came from molasses. The savings ran into millions of dollars, and the new technique greatly simplified production.

Following James Currie's retirement, the highly innovative Kane took over all research and laboratory work for the SUCIAC Department. Years later, he would also play a crucial role in the development of Pfizer's trailblazing work with penicillin. In the meantime, he made substantial improvements in the process used to produce citric acid. At the time, these advances seemed the harbinger of more good news. In 1934, sales rebounded 18 percent and net income rose 53 percent. Pfizer had accomplished what had seemed impossible — the company had remained solvent throughout the Depression without cutting a single member of its workforce.

Pfizer's loyalty to its employees was repaid in 1934 when communist organizers attempted to unionize the factory. A notice signed by the Communist Party and posted in the plant read:

Only through organization will you secure higher wages. When the bosses found out about the Union, they raised the cry, "Communist Union" "Outsiders!" Why? Because they wanted to confuse you, create differences, weaken your ranks and destroy the union. THE COMMUNISTS HAVE NO INTEREST APART FROM THE WORKERS IN YOUR FACTORY!

John Anderson called a special meeting of the board and composed a notice to be posted throughout the plant.

The Management wishes it distinctly understood by all employees in this plant that no objection will be raised if any of the employees wish to join any union or any other organization which the employees may consider will be of benefit to them.

However, it is not necessary for any of our employees to join a union of any kind in order to discuss any matters whatever with the Management, nor will any benefits be secured by joining an outside organization which cannot be secured by free conference with the Management.

Pfizer's open-door policy on communication between employees and management effectively closed the door on the communists' attempts to unionize the plant. The United Chemical Workers Union responded to Anderson's overture by calling a strike, but most employees ignored the union and operations were unaffected.

The First Move Overseas

By 1934, Pfizer's core products — citric acid, cream of tartar, and citrate of lime — were lifting the company onto a higher trajectory of growth. Pfizer was producing all of its domestic citric acid through the SUCIAC process and delivering more than 4 million pounds of citrate of lime to Kemball-Bishop, its new partner in England.

Pfizer and Kemball-Bishop were also finding other ways to join forces. Through a joint venture in 1935, Pfizer agreed to provide the expertise to produce citric acid, while Kemball-Bishop agreed

Above: John L. Smith, right, is shown with John Powers, Sr., in 1935.

Right: Pfizer engineer Dayle McClain, left, seen here with John L. Smith, center, and John McKeen, in 1936, was responsible for building the company's dedicated citric acid plant in record time.

other buildings, and admires. Five months ago, your site was occupied by a shed in decay, and in its place you stand today — a tribute to modern science, a monument to the steadfast purpose, vision, resource, and energy of those who planned and created you. Factory 12 — your creators greet you tonight as a living thing.

The Kemball-Bishop plant was highly efficient. Just how efficient became clear when yields at Factory 12 soon surpassed those at the Brooklyn Works. Smith and McKeen made a hasty trip to England to discover why. They never revealed what they discovered, but each man received a $2,000 bonus, and they incorporated their findings into the U.S. operations. In the meantime, the relationship between Kemball-Bishop and Pfizer prospered. The British firm also became a valued contributor, sending a steady stream of ideas and improvements from Factory 12 to Pfizer headquarters.

As Pfizer strengthened ties with its overseas partner, it also cultivated the talent of its employees at home. John McKeen was a case in point. By the time Pfizer sent him to represent the company overseas, he was already a rising star. Raised in the Flatbush section of Brooklyn, he had studied chemistry and mathematics in preparatory school and during summer vacations had worked as

to build a plant from which Pfizer would receive 20 percent of the profits for two decades.

On November 9, Pfizer engineer Dayle McClain and a new employee, John McKeen, who had joined the company in 1926, set sail for England to oversee the construction of Factory 12 in London. The men supervised crews that worked around the clock, seven days a week, to complete the plant in just five months.

On May 25, 1936, officers of both companies came together for a celebratory dinner at London's Trocadero Restaurant. With spirits high, a Kemball-Bishop officer rose to present a toast to Factory 12:

A prosaic title! The busy world rushes by, sees your graceful and balanced lines towering above

an electrician with the International Brotherhood of Electrical Workers. By his final summer of employment as a journeyman electrician, he was earning the full union wage of $66 a week.

Recognizing Pfizer's potential for greatness and eager to play a part in its prosperity, McKeen, who had earned a degree in chemical engineering at the Polytechnic Institute of Brooklyn, accepted John Smith's and Jasper Kane's offer of employment. Despite a starting salary of $25 a week — less than half of what he had earned as an electrician — McKeen did not hesitate. In his first job at the company, he studied the corrosion problem on Pfizer's stainless steel production equipment, which was rusting as a result of heat and humidity. After spending his first months in overalls, testing and scraping, McKeen recommended a paint with a different base. This solution worked, and the company used the new paint successfully for decades thereafter.

McKeen also worked in the Citric Acid Department, the Miscellaneous Chemical Department, and the Tartaric/Citric Acid Department. In all three places he demonstrated a flair for cost control and for ingenious innovations that spurred productivity. As his tutelage under Smith continued, McKeen also developed many of his mentor's habits, wandering through departments and recording activities in a detailed notebook.

Above: In 1935, Pfizer and Kemball-Bishop joined forces to build this citric acid fermentation plant in London. The plant immediately began achieving higher yields than Pfizer's U.S. plant, prompting John L. Smith and John McKeen to depart for England to find out why.

Below: The dinner celebrating the opening of Kemball-Bishop's SUCIAC plant was attended by John L. Smith, Jasper Kane, John McKeen, and the project's chief engineer, Dayle McClain.

Above: John McKeen joined Pfizer in 1926 for less than half of his salary as an electrician. It was a good move; McKeen worked for Pfizer until retiring in 1968, after 18 years as chairman of the board.

Below: John McKeen, shown quarterbacking his high school football team, spent his first months at Pfizer testing anticorrosive paints. He was so thorough that many people mistook him for a painter.

In 1937, McKeen was promoted to assistant superintendent and moved into an office adjacent to those of John Smith and William Erhart. McKeen's duties ranged from hiring employees to managing quality control, production improvement, and new construction. His increase in responsibilities also coincided with the promotion of the next generation of Pfizer leaders into upper management. The new team included John Davenport, head of the SUCIAC Department; Frank Mead, director of the Tartartic/Citric Acid Department, who was also responsible for the Cream of Tartar and Rochelle shops; and Harry Denzler, who ran the vitamin C project.

Searching for a Cure

By the end of the 1930s, the Great Depression had receded, but war loomed again in Europe. When sales declined in 1938, many plant operations were curtailed or shut down completely. Despite these changes, no jobs were lost, and another attempt to unionize the plant failed.

As the situation in Europe grew more tense, Albert Teeter traveled overseas to set up a new company, the Bureau d'Achat de Tartre Brut de Chas. Pfizer & Company, whose sole business was to purchase crude argols for cream of tartar production.

In 1937, Pfizer put the finishing touches on its third SUCIAC plant, Building 21B, located on the quickly growing Pfizer Brooklyn campus.

When the Spanish Civil War disrupted the delivery of supplies, Italian companies halted the sale of argols and began manufacturing tartrates themselves. Trying to protect itself against further disruptions, Pfizer bought heavily in the argol market, shipping more than 15 million pounds to the United States in 1938.

After Germany invaded Poland in 1939 and World War II erupted, Europe's industrial complex fell into disarray. As millions of troops mobilized to fight and Europe faced the prospect of a lengthy conflict, the search for an effective drug to combat infections became increasingly important. Penicillin's ability to kill bacteria held great promise, but in the years since its discovery by Alexander Fleming in 1928, no one had been able to produce it in large quantities. Pfizer — with its expertise in deep-tank fermentation — was well positioned to come to the rescue. During the next decade, the world would be engulfed in war, but, ironically, the war against infection would take a giant leap forward.

In the early 1940s, Pfizer used flasks to ferment penicillin. As the company's expertise increased, fermentation moved from flasks to fermentation tanks.

1946: Pfizer buys a surplus U.S. government submarine shipyard in Groton, Connecticut, and builds the world's largest citric acid fermentation plant.

1950: Terramycin, a broad-spectrum antibiotic that is the result of the company's first discovery program, becomes the first pharmaceutical sold in the United States under the Pfizer label. Pfizer expands into overseas markets, and the International Division is created.

1952: Pfizer establishes an Agriculture Division, devoted to offering cutting-edge solutions to animal health problems. The division opens its first dedicated research facility in Terre Haute, Indiana.

1949: Pfizer celebrates its 100th anniversary.

1951: By 1951, Pfizer operations are established in Belgium, Brazil, Canada, Cuba, England, Mexico, Panama, and Puerto Rico.

1953: J.B. Roerig and Company, specialists in nutritional supplements, becomes a division of Pfizer. Today, Roerig is an integral part of Pfizer's outstanding Marketing Division.

SECTION II

❧

I N ITS FIRST CENTURY, PFIZER HAD carved out a niche in the fine-chemicals market and had grown at an impressive rate. Yet in 1940, Charles Pfizer & Company was still primarily a chemical manufacturing firm. With the exception of the breakthroughs Pfizer pioneered in fermentation technology, research was not its main focus.

However, Pfizer's achievement in fermentation processes opened the door to new possibilities. No other company in the world matched Pfizer's expertise and confidence in this area.

Although the company's management began to apply these skills to new chemicals, these early successes paled in comparison to one few could predict. With the discovery of penicillin and the subsequent outbreak of a second world war, Pfizer entered a critical era in its history and made another significant contribution to humanity.

1954: Tetracyn, the first purely synthetic broad-spectrum antibiotic discovered by Pfizer researchers, is marketed.

1955: A fermentation plant opens in England, laying the foundation for Pfizer's research and development in Great Britain. Pfizer partners with Japan's Taito and acquires full ownership of the company in 1983.

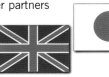

1960: The company signals its increasing commitment to research with the opening of medical research laboratories in Groton, Connecticut.

1961: Pfizer begins a decade of substantial growth and establishes its World Headquarters in midtown Manhattan.

1963: Pfizer purchases Desitin Chemical Company, Inc. Today, Desitin is one of the Consumer Health Care Group's six leading over-the-counter brands, which also include Visine eye drops, Cortizone anti-itch medicines, BenGay analgesics, Unisom sleep aids, and RID pediculicides.

1971: The Central Research Division is established, combining pharmaceutical, agricultural, and chemical R&D worldwide. It eventually includes laboratories in England, France, and Japan, as well as the United States.

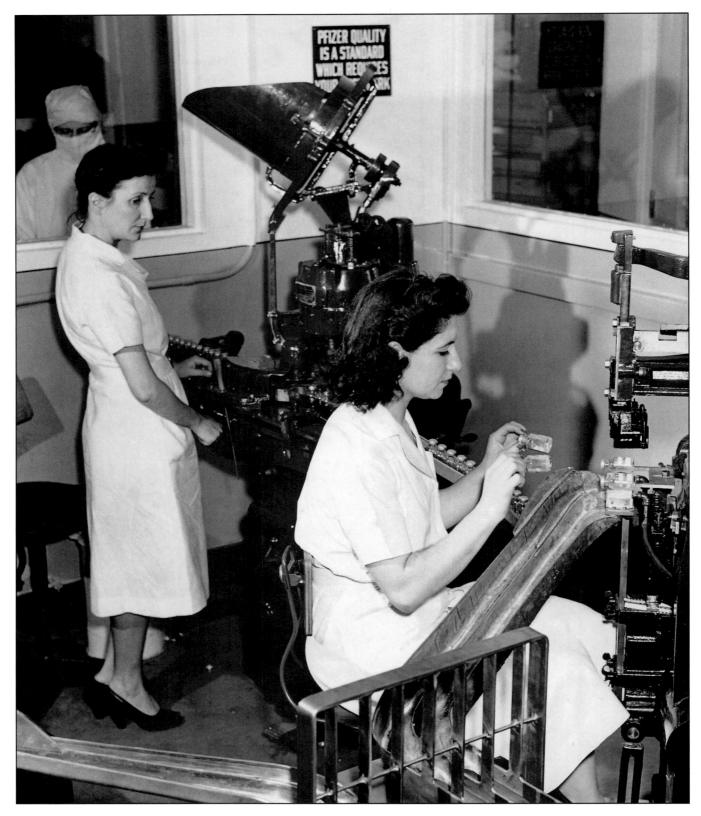

Placards at the Brooklyn plant reminded employees, like these on the penicillin labeling line, that "Pfizer Quality Is A Standard Which Requires Your Best Work." Other placards read, "Preserve Life With Pfizer Penicillin" and "Purest Penicillin Best Resists Germ Invasion."

CHAPTER SIX

THE MAGIC BULLET

1940–1941

Until the late 1930s, few believed that infectious diseases of bacterial origin could be treated using chemical agents.

— Dr. Gladys Hobby, 1985

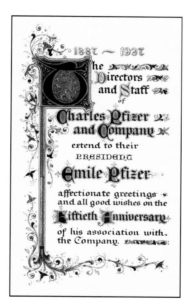

AS THE WAR SWEPT ACROSS Europe in 1940, tragedy also befell Pfizer, taking the lives of its three top leaders. On July 30, 1940, Chairman William H. Erhart suffered a massive heart attack and died at his summer home in Lawrence, Long Island. The quiet 71-year-old, always more comfortable at the Brooklyn Works than in the board room, had spent 51 years at the company that his father had cofounded. The publication *Oil, Paint & Drug Reporter* eulogized Erhart as "keenly interested not only in the company's development but in the welfare of all those connected with the company, and beloved by all."

Barely two months later, the company suffered a second loss with the death of John Anderson, the man whose rise from office boy to chairman exemplified the "American dream." The Brooklyn Works shut down for a day, and the entire company attended Anderson's funeral. In December of 1940, Emile Pfizer was stricken ill and taken to Roosevelt Hospital in New York. Though his own life was ebbing, he devoted all of his energies to his long-held dream for others: the creation of a broad-based employee stock option plan. In a letter dated February 4, 1941, Pfizer outlined his plan to George Anderson, stressing that "the broader the distribution to employees the better."

Pfizer drew up a will stipulating that his shares of Pfizer stock be sold directly to the company. After he died on July 19, 1941, his will generously rewarded loyal employees with cash gifts. He bequeathed more than $235,000 to 244 company employees, many of whom he did not know personally. Pfizer's gifts ranged from $4,000 to each of 24 employees who had been with the company for more than 25 years to $250 apiece given to 108 of their fellow workers. No company officers were included in his bequests. Although he had been formal and restrained during his life, the bequests in Emile Pfizer's will demonstrated the depth of his affection for Pfizer employees and showed a heart as big as the corporation itself.

Even after this distribution, however, Emile Pfizer's estate still retained a large portion of the company stock. Under an agreement he had made in 1920 with William Erhart and John Anderson, none of them could sell, assign or transfer their

---

The certificate was presented to Emile Pfizer in 1937 on the occasion of his 50th anniversary with the company his father cofounded.

Above: George Anderson kept his father's legacy alive when he was elected president of Pfizer in early 1942.

Inset: Pfizer stock first went on the New York Stock Exchange on June 22, 1942. The initial offering was 240,000 shares of common stock made available by George Anderson.

common stock without giving the other two a six-month option to purchase it on a pro-rata basis. When William Erhart died, Emile Pfizer and George Anderson exercised their option to purchase Erhart's 25,200 shares, which represented 21 percent of the company's common stock. Following Emile Pfizer's death and the distribution of his shares to Pfizer employees, George Anderson turned his attention to the late Emile Pfizer's remaining 40,320 shares.

Passing up the opportunity to purchase this stock himself, Anderson persuaded the board to permit Pfizer officers and employees to buy it. The board even encouraged employees to borrow from the company to finance their purchases. Despite these extraordinarily favorable terms, a large surplus of shares remained unsold.

Pfizer Goes Public

At that juncture, Anderson and the board took a historic step: They decided to sell the outstand-ing shares to the public and authorized a recapi-talization plan. After a 3¼-to-1 split, the common and preferred stock were replaced with 631,040 shares of new common stock. On June 22, 1942, Pfizer went public, offering 240,000 shares of the new common stock at $24.75 per share.

George Anderson's skillful and generous lead-ership in these financial dealings convinced the board that it should honor John Anderson's wish that his son head the company. On January 8, 1942, George Anderson was elected president of Pfizer. At the same meeting, John L. Smith was elected senior vice president, and John J. Powers was again elected vice president. In a move simi-lar to a sports team retiring a number, the board honored the memories of William Erhart, Emile

Pfizer, and John Anderson by choosing not to elect a chairman.

Despite Pfizer's loss of three great leaders, 1941 was a banner year for the company. Propelled by wartime demand, both sales and earnings set new records. In his January 29, 1942, letter to the Brooklyn Works employees, John Smith emphasized that the company's renewed prosperity came at a terrible price: "It would have been far better for all of us to have never encountered this hysterical demand for materials and instead to have been able to continue our efforts to develop our business and solve our problems in normal fashion."

The Magic Bullet Is Found

But out of these perilous times came an achievement that would save the lives of millions and mark the dawn of modern medicine — the successful mass production of a magic bullet called penicillin. This antibiotic had been discovered more than a decade earlier on a September day in 1928, when British bacteriologist Alexander Fleming returned to his London laboratory to find the future of medicine staring at him from a petri dish. A robust culture of staph bacteria was unexpectedly dying. The culprit was a common airborne mold, *penicillium*,

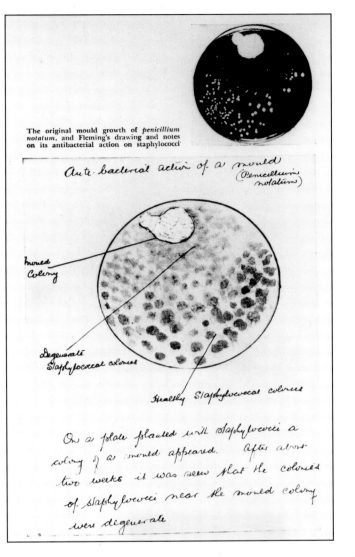

Above: John Powers, Sr., started with Pfizer as a salesman in Chicago and rose to become vice president of Sales. His son, John Powers, Jr., would become one of Pfizer's most influential chairmen.

Above right: Alexander Fleming's original sketch shows a ring of dead staphylococci bacteria surrounding a common mold, which he identified and named *Penicillium notatum*.

Right: Bacteriologist Alexander Fleming, who discovered penicillin in 1928, is portrayed in his London laboratory.

the very fungus that had plagued the development of SUCIAC at Pfizer.

Fleming would prove that juice from the mold could stop killers like pneumonia and scarlet fever stone cold. But to his chagrin, he also found that the active substance, which he called penicillin, was difficult to extract and impossible to preserve. After a year's research, Fleming shelved his discovery in frustration. He later observed, "It is the lone worker who makes the first advance ... but as the world becomes more complicated, we are less and less able to carry anything through ... without the collaboration of others."

A decade later, a team of scientists at Oxford University led by physiologist Ernest Chain and bio-

chemist Howard Florey rediscovered Fleming's work and revived research into the disease-killing mold. Chain and Florey managed to produce sufficient quantities to determine that penicillin injections killed numerous bacterial infections in mice, rats, and cats.

Chain and Florey also published their findings in the August 24, 1940, issue of the prestigious British medical

Above: From left, Lord Howard Florey, Ernest Chain, and Harold Raistrick. Raistrick began working with penicillin in 1931 and confirmed many of Fleming's findings. Florey and Chain picked up the thread in 1941 at Oxford University.

Below: In 1941, at the American Society for Clinical Investigation, Martin Dawson of Columbia University delivered a paper on the penicillin work done at the university. Attending doctors heralded the dawn of a new age in the fight against bacterial infection.

journal *Lancet*, creating a sensation throughout the scientific community. However, with England under aerial bombardment, the scientists at Oxford could conduct only limited tests. Armed with increasing evidence of the remarkable powers of penicillin, the Oxford team sought help in the United States.

Meanwhile, the horrors of war had convinced Americans that penicillin's potential could not be ignored. At Columbia University's College of Physicians and Surgeons in New York City, Dr. Martin Henry Dawson contacted Chain and requested a mold sample from the Oxford University laboratory. Within two months, Dawson and his team were administering doses of crudely processed penicillin to patients at Presbyterian Hospital in New York City. The doses were too small to completely eradicate bacterial endocarditis, but nonetheless, the doctors noticed a substantial

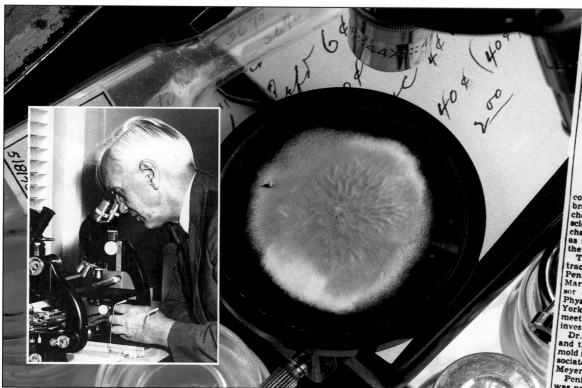

Above: Artifacts from the early phase of penicillin development include handwritten notes by Alexander Fleming, a mold colony, and an ampule. Inset: Fleming at work in his laboratory.

Right: Microbiologist Gladys Hobby joined Pfizer in 1944 and spent the next 15 years helping to develop penicillin and other antibiotics, such as streptomycin and Terramycin. Prior to joining Pfizer, Hobby was part of the Columbia University research team that prepared the first penicillin specifically for treatment of infection.

reduction of the infectious organism in blood samples taken following treatment with the new drug.

Properly processed, penicillin could cure virulent infections. Dawson and his team presented these findings May 5, 1941, at the meeting of the American Society for Clinical Investigation in Atlantic City. Pfizer officers John Davenport and Gordon Cragwell were among those in attendance. Inspired by the possibility of saving lives and of producing the world's first "wonder drug," they offered Pfizer's assistance.

One of the greatest chapters in the history of the company was about to begin. Other pharmaceutical companies, including Merck and Squibb, also threw their hats into the ring, and the historic high-stakes race to mass-produce a life-saving new drug was on.

Phila. Evening Bulletin

MAY 5 - 1941 Fees

THE EVENING

GERM KILLER FOUND IN COMMON MOLD

Physician says Penicillin may Prove more Useful than Sulfanilamides

By STEVEN M. SPENCER
(Of The Bulletin Staff)

Atlantic City, May 5.—From a common mold which grows on stale bread and which gives Roquefort cheese its highly prized green color scientists have prepared a germ-chasing medicine which "may prove as useful or even more useful than the sulfanilamide drugs."

This appraisal of penicillin, extracted from the mold known as Penicillium, was made today by Dr. Martin H. Dawson, associate professor of medicine in the College of Physicians and Surgeons, New York, speaking at the 33d annual meeting of the society for clinical investigation, at Haddon Hall.

Dr. Dawson reported experiments and treatments conducted with the mold medicine by himself and his associates, Drs. Gladys L. Hobby, Karl Meyer and Eleanor Chaffee.

Penicillin was first prepared and was named by Dr. Fleming in England, who noticed that a colony of staphylococcus germs accidentally contaminated with spores of penicillium did not grow. This was in 1929 and not much work was done with the material until last year, although now many Englishmen are chasing "strep" and other germs in the nasal passages by using the dried penicillin as a snuff, Dr. Dawson said.

The material, as tested on animals and in a few human cases, appears to produce no toxic effects when given in doses far beyond those necessary to clear up infections, Dr. Dawson reported. This would be a distinct advantage over the sulfanilamide drugs, which are toxic to some people. And the mold medicine is effective against all the germs of the Gram-positive classification, which includes streptococcus, staphylococcus, meningococcus, the pneumonia germs, and many others. It is slightly effective against the Gram-negative bacteria. Dr. Dawson believes it has "unlimited possibilities."

Another medicine obtained from a microscopic form of life, gramicidin from a bacillus found in the soil, has been highly effective in the treatment of ulcerating sores of the leg and other parts of the body as well as in bladder infections and empyema (pus in the chest cavity), it was reported today.

The soil bacillus preparation, isolated two years ago by Dr. Rene Dubos, of the Rockefeller Institute for Medical Research, must not be given by vein, however, Dr. Wallace E. Harrell, of the Mayo Clinic, warned, as it causes breakdown of the red blood cells. Dr. Harrell and his associate, Dr. Dorothy Heilman, concluded it was safe for local application, however, as it is not toxic to the flesh itself.

PFIZER

IS

PERFORMING AN

OUTSTANDING SERVICE

AS THE WORLD'S

LARGEST PRODUCER

OF

PENICILLIN

CHAS. PFIZER & CO., INC.

MANUFACTURING CHEMISTS • ESTABLISHED 1849

81 Maiden Lane
New York 7

444 West Grand Ave.
Chicago 10

Chemicals For Those Who Serve Man's Well-Being

Throughout the war, Pfizer's penicillin production steadily increased until the company could boast it was the world's largest producer.

CHAPTER SEVEN

PERFECTING THE PROCESS
1942–1945

The mold is as temperamental as an opera singer, the yields are low, the isolation difficult, the extraction murder, the purification invites disaster. Think of the risks.

— John L. Smith, 1942

WITH ITS WORLD LEADERship in fermentation technology, Pfizer and penicillin production were a natural match. Wasting no time, Jasper Kane and Gordon Cragwell began working with the research team from Columbia University. The first experiments with penicillin were classic Pfizer — using surface fermentation in glass flasks. Unfortunately, the yields were exceedingly low.

John McKeen recalled those first penicillin trials:

We worked in the old research laboratories with these flasks developed by Pfizer. They were easily contaminated, and the content of the penicillin wasn't very much more than specks in sea water. A few parts per million were extremely dilute, and it was a very involved process to get an impure product, which no one knew how to analyze. We had to put this impure penicillin into laboratory animals to make sure it would not harm anyone.

Then we went up into the citric units at the SUCIAC plant and borrowed that technology and some large glass flasks for bigger-scale production.... In these citric units, we could better control the temperature and humidity.

The large flasks were an improvement over the other containers that had been tried and discarded, and John L. Smith even suggested using milk bottles. This approach was scrapped, however, as soon as the company realized that the cost of sterilizing and pasteurizing thousands of bottles with microscopic yields would be prohibitive. Flat citric pans were more cost effective, but the contamination problem was still staggering. Yields varied from 20 units per cc to nothing at all.

Pfizer was in the ironic position of trying to turn an old enemy into a new friend. The company was striving to cultivate the very mold that had plagued it for decades. In the early days of citric acid fermentation, Pfizer had lost many batches to a troublesome pest that turned out to be penicillin mold, and now company scientists were trying to grow penicillin for its own sake.

Despite these obstacles, by late 1941, Pfizer was making small daily deliveries of penicillin fermentation liquor to Drs. Martin Henry Dawson, Karl Meyer, and Gladys Hobby at Columbia University. The liquor was so fragile that samples frequently

---

Researchers worked with many kinds of penicillin mold, including *Penicillium chrysogenum*, to find the most efficient one. This strain was found to work especially well in a deep-tank environment.

Above: Alexander Fleming discovered the penicillin mold in 1928 but had trouble attracting attention to his find. Gladys Hobby, who was part of the team that introduced penicillin to the world in 1941, later helped Pfizer develop Terramycin, the company's first proprietary antibiotic.

Below: Penicillin G, a product of *Penicillium chrysogenum* fermentation, was what scientists were looking for, but it was prone to contamination.

Inset: Oxford University scientist Norman Heatley is credited with developing a way to increase penicillin yields in 1941, at the same time that Howard Florey was completing the first clinical trials. During the war, Heatley traveled with Florey to the United States.

perished during the brief taxi ride from Brooklyn to Columbia University in Manhattan.

The Pfizer-Columbia University venture was being monitored closely in Washington. Hitler's nightly bombing raids on London precluded experiments there, and the British appealed to the United States for help. When, in the summer of 1941, the Committee on Medical Research met in Washington, D.C., the meeting was attended by representatives from Pfizer, Merck, Lederle, Squibb, the U.S. Department of Agriculture, Johns Hopkins University, and the National Defense Research Council.

President Roosevelt asked the attendees to make the acceleration of penicillin production their highest priority. He urged the companies to avoid duplication by embracing cooperation and communication, putting aside all patent issues. Adopting an all-for-one, one-for-all attitude was, however, easier said than done. In addition to urging every chemical company to join in this effort, the government also expected competitors like Pfizer, Merck, and Squibb to share confidential information with everyone who wanted it.

Pfizer had additional concerns. The company's experience in fermentation convinced it that penicillium molds could be extremely hazardous. Until Pfizer was sure that it could avoid contaminating its other fermented products, the company intended to proceed cautiously.

The British and Penicillin Fever

In October 1941, in the midst of this "penicillin fever," Oxford scientists Howard Florey and Norman Heatley traveled to the United States. Their arrival fanned the flames of public and scientific interest in the "miracle drug," and they tried to persuade U.S. pharmaceutical companies to do what their war-torn British counterparts could not do: commit huge sums of money to fund the R&D necessary to mass-produce penicillin.

During his visit to New York City, Florey spoke at the prestigious University Club, where John McKeen was in attendance. McKeen wrote, "Dr. Florey told us about the

Above: Scientists at Chester County Mushroom Laboratories in Pennsylvania were among the early collaborators in the effort to produce penicillin. They used their expertise in mushroom cultivation to surface ferment penicillin in case Pfizer's experiments with deep-tank fermentation did not produce results.

Below: Penicillin, shown during surface fermentation in large flasks, was prone to contamination by the enzyme penicillinase.

Oxford group's work with penicillin. Several military officers afterward impressed upon us the importance of getting additional supplies of penicillin. I returned to speak to our team at Pfizer, and we agreed to go ahead and put a very concerted effort behind it."

On December 7, 1941, the Japanese bombed Pearl Harbor, and the United States immediately declared war on Japan. Ten days later, the Committee on Medical Research convened in Washington and addressed the urgent need for penicillin. By the time the meeting adjourned, the participants were united in their common mission. They differed, however, on the best means to reach their goal. Merck and Squibb believed that once the molecular structure of penicillin was determined, it could be synthetically manufactured, much as sulfa drugs were.

Pfizer believed that fermentation was the answer. Throughout most of 1942, however,

extracting usable penicillin seemed more frustrating and less productive than panning for gold. Pfizer was producing only 55 liters of fermentation broth per day, or about 300 liters a week. The yields were low, and Pfizer was running neck and neck with Merck and Squibb in recovery.

Penicillin was so scarce in early 1943 that it was available only to the country's top infectious disease specialists. Even then, supplies were barely sufficient to conduct proper field trials. Nonetheless, when the War Production Board assumed control of all penicillin distribution in the summer of 1943, the power and efficacy of the drug were no longer in question.

In an early example of a media feeding frenzy, a deluge of stories about the "miracle drug" produced a public outcry for penicillin. One vial of it was rumored to fetch as much as $150,000 on the black market. Security was so tight that an armed military escort accompanied the transport of all Pfizer penicillin.

Smith's Angel

If there had been a poster child for penicillin, it would have to have been the young girl stricken by subacute bacterial endocarditis who lay dying in a Brooklyn hospital in 1943. John Smith had become acquainted with the girl's physician, Dr. Leo Loewe of the Brooklyn Jewish Hospital, well before the government had decreed that all penicillin be reserved for the front lines.

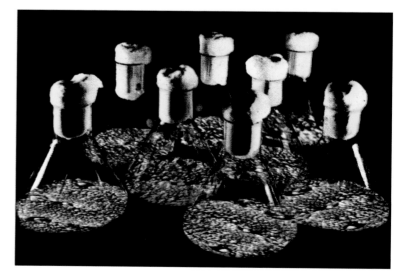

THE 'PENICILLIN GIRL'

FOR 15-YEAR-OLD SHIRLEY CARTER, what started in September 1943 as little more than a bothersome sore throat while on a family fishing trip to Florida soon turned dramatically worse. By the time she returned to her hometown, Macon, Georgia, she was running a blistering 105-degree fever.

For three days, her fever raged without relief. She was taken to Middle Georgia Hospital, where the attending physician, Dr. Herbert Weaver, gave her the standard treatment for strep throat: ice packs and aspirin for the

After her life was saved in 1943 with Pfizer penicillin, Anne Shirley Carter, who later became Shirley Olsson, went on to become a doctor. *(Photo credit: Breton Littlehales.)*

fever and sulfa drugs for the strep. Nothing helped. Her temperature soared to a life-threatening 107 degrees, and her lymph nodes swelled like balloons.

As her condition deteriorated, she remembered reading an article in *Reader's Digest* about a new miracle drug, penicillin, which she mentioned to her father and to Dr. Weaver. Her physician agreed that the drug would be wonderful if it could be found. Shirley's father, C.K. Carter, replied, "I'll find a way to get it."

With the help of *The Macon News*, C.K. Carter launched a nationwide search. It led to Pfizer, but the company could not release the penicillin until a Boston physician, Dr. Chester Keefer, who was in charge of determining civilian use of the new drug, gave his approval. Fortunately, as Shirley Carter would later recall, Dr. Keefer quickly sent a telegram giving his consent. The staff at *The Macon News* contacted the Army Air Corps and secured the use of a B-24 Liberator bomber to rush the drug from Pfizer to the dying girl. The plane flew the drug to Macon on September 5, and the local police escorted the shipment to the hospital, where it was administered immediately. During treatment, the desperately ill patient developed trench mouth and her teeth loosened, but her fever finally began to abate. By September 21, the young girl who had lingered so close to death was able to go home.

Carter says that this dramatic experience encouraged her to enter the field of internal medicine. After graduating from the Medical College of Virginia, she practiced in Richmond, where she met her husband and eventually raised four children. Now retired and living in West Point, Virginia, Carter says that she remains forever grateful to the work and research performed by penicillin's founder, Dr. Alexander Fleming, and to Pfizer: "Dr. Fleming was brilliant to recognize a fluke when he saw it on his culture dish," she says. "And I owe the rest to Pfizer."

When Dr. Loewe hooked up his patient to a three-day intravenous penicillin drip, the results were amazing. For part of the time, Smith and John McKeen sat at the girl's bedside, anxiously watching her progress. They were stunned to see the color return to her face as she began to recover from a disease that killed most of its victims. The medical community was also shocked, but there was a simple explanation: Doctors treating other patients had not been using enough penicillin, whereas Loewe had dripped 40,000 units into his young patient.

Right: As Pfizer's expertise increased, the company moved from surface fermentation in flasks to deep-tank fermentation.

Below right: The fermentation room shown in 1942, when penicillin was surface fermented in thousands of glass flasks.

Below left: In the Pfizer penicillin drying room, batteries of driers were used to turn vials of concentrated broth into powder.

As production expanded in all its businesses, Pfizer steadily took over new land and buildings around the Brooklyn plant.

Smith continued sending penicillin to Dr. Loewe until he was ordered to ship all supplies to the military. But that order didn't stop people from getting sick, and Loewe continued to ask him for the life-saving drug. Determined to help, Smith shipped him much of the 8 million units of penicillin that the government allotted Pfizer each month for research.

Although Pfizer continued to make incremental gains in penicillin production throughout 1942, overall yields remained frustratingly low. Realizing that brewing penicillin in small flasks could never yield the tremendous volume needed, Jasper Kane decided that desperate times called for desperate measures. He proposed that the company attempt to produce penicillin using the same deep-tank fermentation methods it had perfected for the production of citric acid. Kane's proposal was as risky as it was radical. It would require that Pfizer curtail production of citric acid and other well-established products while it focused on the development of penicillin. It would also risk contamination of the company's existing fermentation facilities.

In Smith's opinion, the proposal was fraught with peril. As he remarked, "The mold is as temperamental as an opera singer, the yields are low, the isolation difficult, the extraction murder, the purification invites disaster. Think of the risks.... Think of what it means if you lose a 2,000-gallon tank as against what you lose if a flask goes bad. Is it worth it?"

Kane recognized the risks but saw no alternative. He was convinced that deep-tank fermentation was the only way to mass-produce penicillin. He asked for a decision. On a cool fall night in the boardroom in Brooklyn, John L. Smith presented the choice to Pfizer's managers and shareholders.

Despite the risks, the company voted overwhelmingly to go ahead. The Pfizer team, managers and workers alike, voted to invest millions of dollars, putting their own assets as Pfizer shareholders at stake to buy the equipment and facilities for deep-tank fermentation. On September 20, Pfizer purchased the nearby, defunct Rubel Ice Plant. Employees worked around the clock, seven days a week, to convert it and to perfect the complex production process. John L. Smith posted a sign in the plant that read, "The faster this building is completed ... the quicker our wounded men get penicillin, the new life-saving drug."

The World's First Penicillin Plant

Wartime restrictions made construction a nightmare. With building materials strictly rationed, McKeen had to scramble for every rivet and bolt. A used elevator from Long Island, a secondhand boiler from Indiana — piece by piece, Pfizer cobbled together the manufacturing plant in just four short months.

On March 1, Pfizer made history. It opened the doors of the world's first penicillin plant. With fourteen 7,500-gallon tanks and facilities for recovery, purification, and concentration, Pfizer soon was producing five times more penicillin than originally anticipated. Kane estimated that he would be able to produce up to 45 million units a month, an astounding achievement that had been made possible by impeccable organization, leadership, and teamwork.

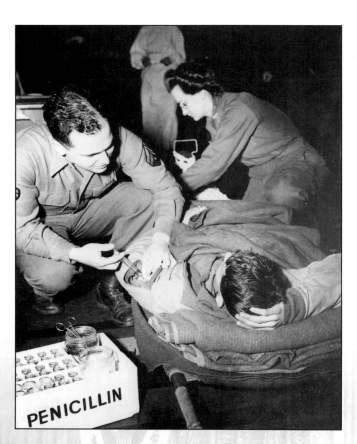

Pfizer's success was the product of many small refinements and adjustments carried out by a staff with extensive experience in the submerged fermentation of other molds. To participants, the day-by-day progress had seemed agonizingly slow, but to outsiders, Pfizer's breakthrough seemed to come in the blink of an eye — almost like going from the invention of the wheel to the automobile overnight. Pfizer blazed a trail in penicillin production that its rivals could only follow.

Recognizing the superiority of the Pfizer process and desperate for massive quantities of penicillin, the U.S. government authorized 19 companies to produce the antibiotic using Pfizer's deep-tank fermentation techniques — which the company had agreed to share with its competitors.

Left: Penicillin was a blessing on the battlefield, where it could knock out the infections that plagued armies in wartime.

Below: In 1943, Pfizer's contributions to the war effort were rewarded with the Army-Navy "E" Award. Pfizer's president, George Anderson, is second from left, and his successor, John L. Smith, is at the far right.

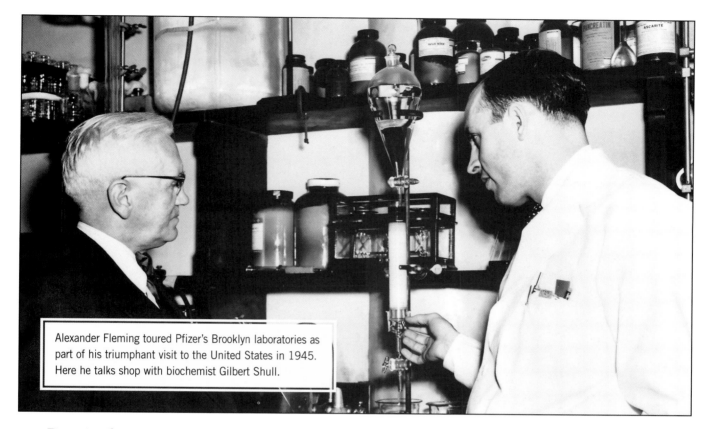

Alexander Fleming toured Pfizer's Brooklyn laboratories as part of his triumphant visit to the United States in 1945. Here he talks shop with biochemist Gilbert Shull.

Despite their access to Pfizer's technology, however, none of these companies could rival the quality or quantity of the product turned out by Pfizer. Although much smaller in size than many of its competitors, Pfizer produced 90 percent of the penicillin that went ashore with Allied forces at Normandy, France, on D-Day. For the rest of the war, Pfizer produced more of the wonder drug than all the other manufacturers combined. As supplies grew to meet demand, hundreds of thousands of people, both on the front lines and on the home front, could testify to the life-saving power of Pfizer's antibiotic.

The company's vital contribution to the war effort was heralded around the nation. Pfizer earned the coveted Army-Navy "E" Award on April 17, 1943, for excellence in war production. The award was presented on May 24 to a group of 800 Pfizer employees gathered in Building 22 at the Brooklyn Works.

In a July 4, 1944, letter to John L. Smith, Major General George Lull, deputy surgeon general of the War Department, lauded Pfizer's extraordinary accomplishments:

The outstanding performance of your organization in the production of penicillin has been a major factor in satisfying military needs for this vital drug. The United States Army congratulates Chas. Pfizer & Company on this splendid record and expresses its deep appreciation for the service rendered by the world's largest producer of penicillin.

At a time in history when much was demanded of Americans in the name of freedom, this was perhaps one of Pfizer's finest hours. Pfizer's hard-won victories in penicillin production also translated into record growth of the company's bottom line. Wartime contracts contributed to sales of $24.4 million, up 46 percent from the previous year's record. Net earnings in 1944 rose to $2.3 million, an increase of 31 percent from 1943's earnings of $1.7 million. As the war came to an end, Pfizer had been sorely tested and had shown itself more than equal to the task. In the postwar world, it remained to be seen what path the company would chart with its hard-won scientific victory.

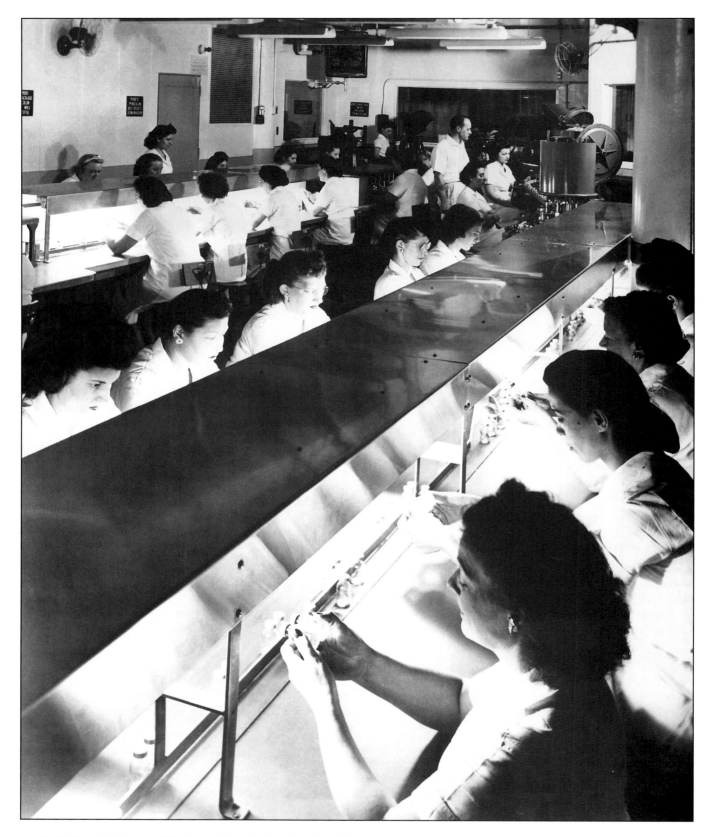

Penicillin quickly became Pfizer's most important product. Shown here is the packaging line in the Brooklyn penicillin plant, about 1945.

CHAPTER EIGHT

NEW PLANTS AND NEW MARKETS

1945–1949

If you want to go broke in a hurry, just go into the penicillin business.

— John McKeen, 1978

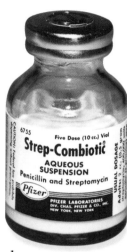

DURING THE WAR YEARS, PFIZER transformed itself from a supplier of chemicals into a pharmaceutical company that sold products under its own label. For almost 100 years, Pfizer had sold its products in bulk to other businesses, which then sold them under their own brand names. After Pfizer developed and perfected the mass production of penicillin, however, its leaders realized that the company had the potential to do much more.

By the end of World War II, production time for penicillin G had been reduced from 13 days to 4 days, and production was pushed to the limit to meet worldwide demand. With materials and equipment stacked in every corner of the Brooklyn Works, teams of engineers and scientists continually refined their approach.

The work environment was intense and frenetic, but extremely productive. As Pfizer fermentation expert Ernst Weber observed, "Every tank was sort of a large-scale experiment. It was the secret to Pfizer's success."

Although penicillin was the company's most important product, citric acid remained a staple, with output rising from 13.6 million pounds in 1939 to 25.1 million in 1944. When, in 1946, Pfizer installed additional equipment on the second floor of the SUCIAC building, the company easily exceeded the 30-million-pound mark.

Good Times, New Leaders … and New Headquarters

Midway through the 1940s, the Pfizer board elected George Anderson chairman, John L. Smith president, and John McKeen vice president. They promptly turned their attention to opportunities for expansion. In the first half of the decade, Pfizer had been operating beyond planned capacity at its various Brooklyn facilities. Now that the war was over, the company was free to build.

At the same time, a debate broke out between two Pfizer factions that was reminiscent of the rivalry between the Brooklyn Dodgers and the New York Giants. One group within senior management, led by John L. Smith and John McKeen, believed that the time had come to shut down 81 Maiden Lane. Vigorously opposing McKeen and Smith, however, was the Pfizer "old guard," led by George Anderson, who had worked in Manhattan on Maiden Lane his entire career. The conflict was largely generational, but as John L. Smith pointed out in a memo to George Anderson, "the greatest

In 1948, Pfizer became the largest producer of the antibiotic streptomycin. Pfizer enhanced streptomycin's effectiveness by combining it with penicillin, creating a medicine that was called Strep-Combiotic.

benefits can be achieved by bringing the entire New York organization to Brooklyn, and we will sacrifice in efficiency if we do otherwise."

The debate continued until 1948, when a compromise was struck officially moving Pfizer's headquarters to Brooklyn but still maintaining a presence on Maiden Lane. The Pfizer sales staff argued — sensibly — that without a Manhattan office, clients from overseas would have to travel all the way to Brooklyn to meet with company representatives. With Pfizer's exports steadily rising, the sales team not only carried the day but also got permission to establish its own export division — under Donald Hilton's direction.

Left: Despite the excitement surrounding penicillin, Pfizer retained its position as the leading producer of citric acid. Taken in 1948, this picture shows the large fermentation tanks in the Brooklyn plant.

Below: Building 16, built in 1947 at the Brooklyn Works, housed administration, operations, and personnel, in addition to the plant hospital.

Meanwhile, in Brooklyn, plans were made to tear down older warehouses and construct Building 16, an eight-story facility west of Warehouse A on the south side of Flushing Avenue. This new building housed everything from the plant hospital and dispensary to the loading docks. It also included additional warehouse space, a cafeteria, employee locker rooms, and research facilities for the expanding Biochemical Division.

For all its advantages, Building 16 in Brooklyn could not overcome one persistent problem: New York State water allocations. Pfizer's monthly allotment of 86 million gallons from local wells was non-negotiable. With no additional water allocations from the city and current operations quickly approaching peak capacity, the company needed new supplies. Pfizer charged real estate agent Carl Buerman and Jack Powers, the son of Pfizer's retired vice president, John Powers, Sr., with finding a new site for production.

Hired in 1941, the younger Powers had been the first lawyer to join Pfizer. After Smith became company president in 1945, Powers served as his assistant. In Samuel Mines' 1978 book, *Pfizer ... An Informal History*, Jack Powers recalled

Sir Alexander Fleming maintained a close relationship with Pfizer. On June 26, 1945, he posed with many of the company's officers for this photo. John Powers, Jr., future president of Pfizer, is fourth from the left. Also pictured, left to right, are J.C. Blagg, Bill Stuart, Al Finlay, Jasper Kane, Jack Goett, Dayle McClain, Fleming, Richard Pasternack, John Davenport, Ray Patelski, and J.R. McMahon.

the training that he received at the hands of John L. Smith:

He trained me ... by being extraordinarily tough. We were working on the vitamin A license agreement. This was very important for Pfizer, and he would let me do a great deal of the negotiating.... He'd let me act as both his lawyer and his assistant, and I did a lot of work on this particular agreement. After many months, I remember coming to his office for his signature, and I was a little bit proud of my work. He must have detected it, because I walked in with the licensing agreement.... He looked up, and he was wearing no smile.

"What have you got there?"

I told him I had the licensing agreement for vitamin A, trying to conceal my pride. I was pretty pleased with myself. It was done ahead of time and in perfect order.

"Let me see it," he said. He grabbed the agreement and started reading it. He read a couple of lines and asked, "Have you checked the patent number?"

Now any license agreement will start out with a "whereas" clause which will say, "Whereas so and so owns patent number such and such for the production of vitamin A," and goes on. So after reading just this opening whereas clause, he said to me, "Have you checked the patent number?"

It was such an extraordinary question! After months of working on this thing. Of course we were talking about the right patent. I kind of stumbled, and he said, "Well, did you?"

I said, "I'm sure it's been checked."

"I didn't ask you that. Did you personally check this number?"

"Well, as a matter of fact, no."

"Take this out of my office. Go back to the library and check the patent number and don't dare come in here asking me to sign an important license agreement without having checked the patent number!"

That was John L. Smith. He knew I was furious. He never apologized or kidded about it or in any way softened it. He knew I went out of his office boiling mad. I nearly walked into the street and kept going. Yet it is tough bosses like that, training like that, that really makes you.

Together, Powers and Buerman searched from Massachusetts to Virginia for a new base of operations. After exploring more than three dozen loca-

Pfizer spent millions to outfit the Groton plant with fermentation tanks for citric acid. John McKeen is seen looking into the tank during a 1948 inspection. Beside him are John L. Smith, in the foreground, and John Davenport, in the middle.

Above: Pfizer officers observe Groton plant employees bagging citric acid.

Right: Pfizer began to build up its Groton facility to produce penicillin as demand increased. Groton had as many as 15 linked fermentation tanks for continuous penicillin output. Shown here are crystallizers.

tions, they found the perfect spot: 28 acres on the Thames River, opposite New London, Connecticut. Called the Groton, Connecticut, Victory Yard, it was a government-owned section of the shipyard operated by the Electric Boat Company. Originally a shipyard operated by the Groton Iron Works in 1917 and 1918, the site was converted to a fish-rendering plant in 1927. During World War II, the government purchased it to build submarines, investing nearly $10 million in constructing the yard and its facilities.

Pfizer could easily convert many of the existing buildings, and the Victory Yard's deepwater port offered a plentiful supply of water for cooling equipment. Before purchasing the property, however, Pfizer still had to persuade the federal government that the company would have a positive impact on the Groton community without taking away jobs or diminishing the tax base in Brooklyn.

Negotiating for Groton

In a February 27, 1946, letter to the War Assets Administration, John L. Smith argued that the government should accept Pfizer's offer since the property had few potential buyers and had not been used for some time. He noted that local officials were particularly troubled that the site would become unproductive, as it had after World War I. To strengthen his case, Smith cited the shortcomings of the Victory Yard, noting that it lacked the essentials for commercial or manufacturing use. Although Smith could not convince government officials to accept Pfizer's initial offer of $801,000, they did reduce the asking price from $1.3 million to just over $909,000. In April 1946, the parties reached agreement, and at the same time, Pfizer bought 59 acres of neighboring land for an additional $120,000.

The company set about turning the abandoned submarine yard into the largest fermentation plant on Earth. John McKeen immediately began building a team to construct a power plant. He also started converting existing buildings to enable them to manufacture citric acid and Pfizer's other leading products. Fortunately, finding skilled employees posed few difficulties. Pfizer's reputation for fairness toward workers and its reputation for quality immediately attracted the necessary recruits.

The company also benefited from an abundance of available employees in the Groton area, many of whom had been laid off by the Electric Boat Company. Overcoming the physical obstacles and governmental red tape, the Groton plant shipped its first order of citric acid from the new facilities in April 1948.

Pfizer was well positioned to finance this ambitious expansion. Sales for 1946 — at $43.6 million — proved to be the best ever, more than a 58 percent increase over the previous year. Net earnings from 1945 to 1946 more than quintupled, with more than half of the growth fueled by demand for penicillin, as well as for citric acid and vitamins.

Pfizer's postwar expansion of its physical plant and its growth in earnings proceeded in tandem with increased production of penicillin, the company's most profitable product. After 18 months of operation, Pfizer's penicillin plant was producing more than 300 billion Oxford units, six times its original capacity. But there was a hitch. Production was proceeding at such a pace that it created a bottleneck in the Packaging Department, where penicillin was carefully freeze-dried in individual vials.

In March 1945, the War Production Board lifted controls on penicillin and released it for civilian use. As producers began to distribute the antibiotic through normal business channels, the cost of a 100,000-Oxford-unit dose of penicillin fell to $1.54. Although prices continued to drop, the required doses decreased more slowly. Once in the body, penicillin rapidly disappeared. This meant that large amounts passed through the system without attacking the infection, necessitating continuous injections.

Patients needed to take a minimum of four painful shots daily. To lessen the pain, doctors began mixing dry penicillin with procaine hydrochloride. When they noticed a hard, hazy residue forming in the vials after procaine

The first shipments of citric acid left the Groton plant in April 1948.

hydrochloride was added, the hospitals returned the vials to Pfizer for analysis, believing they were somehow spoiled.

Pfizer's Analytical and Research departments, however, soon made a fortuitous discovery. This residue was actually crystallized penicillin G plus procaine. Far less soluble, crystalline penicillin G not only lived longer in the body — which meant fewer shots — it also significantly diminished the pain of injections. Not surprisingly, demand for this form of penicillin took off, and the price plummeted to 31 cents for a 100,000-Oxford-unit vial.

Ironically, the wartime spirit of cooperation that had led Pfizer to share the secrets of penicillin production with the entire industry now jeopardized the company. Pfizer executives were dismayed to see partners become competitors as companies that had once bought and resold antibiotics made by Pfizer built their own plants and began making their own penicillin. Customers canceled orders by the truckload, and penicillin began to pile up at Pfizer's Marcy Avenue building in Brooklyn.

Streptomycin

If the company was to hold its place in the vanguard of modern medicine, it needed a breakthrough. That came in the form of a new candidate — streptomycin, the second antibiotic and the first drug with potential for treating tuberculosis. Discovered in the early 1940s by Selman Waksman at the New Jersey Agricultural Experiment Station, streptomycin originally was targeted for infections that proved resistant to penicillin.

Pfizer began studying streptomycin fermentation in the fall of 1944. The microbiological evaluations were conducted by Ernst Weber, who later became vice president of Research, and Gladys Hobby, who had come to Pfizer from Columbia University to join the Pfizer team that introduced penicillin to the world.

From the outset, Pfizer streptomycin showed unexpected results. Other studies conducted by Pfizer researchers tracked its effective-

ness in fighting typhoid fever. By the end of 1945, Pfizer was shipping vials containing 500 milligrams (500,000 units) of streptomycin to the U.S. Army.

The expertise the company had acquired in working with penicillin enabled the Chemical Research Department to accelerate development of this new drug. Within a few months, Pfizer's team reported a marked improvement over initial batches. Yield rose from 35 units to 100 units per cc.

As Pfizer easily surmounted core problems of potency and production, the company's output far exceeded its obligation to the Army. The question quickly arose as to whether Pfizer should remain a wholesale supplier or compete directly with its current clients. Vice President of Sales Fred Stock recommended that Pfizer continue to distribute streptomycin through other companies, just as it had originally done with penicillin.

Smith disagreed. The race to refine and market streptomycin was not confined to Pfizer. Merck, Parke-Davis, Upjohn, Abbott, Lederle, Lilly, Squibb, and Schenley had all participated in government-sponsored clinical studies, and they were determined to develop the antibiotic using Pfizer's fermentation techniques.

By the end of 1946, wholesale costs had dropped precipitously. The price of a gram vial of streptomycin, which had cost $16 in 1945, fell more than 50 percent. But when research revealed, in 1947, that streptomycin could also combat urinary tract infections, demand skyrocketed.

The Move to Vigo

Pfizer recognized that it would need a third plant — one devoted exclusively to producing antibiotics, particularly streptomycin — to keep up with demand. The company purchased a plant, called Vigo, in December 1947,

Ernst M. Weber, who would later become vice president of Research for Pfizer, worked on early experiments to produce penicillin through deep-tank fermentation and helped prepare the first batches of streptomycin.

in Terre Haute, Indiana. Unlike the Groton Victory Yard, Vigo was a 700-acre state-of-the-art facility designed and built by the U.S. Army. The site seemed ideally suited for work with fermentation and lacked only the facilities for recovery and antibiotic processing.

John McKeen submitted a formal proposal to the Army Corps of Engineers emphasizing the company's goal of producing antibiotics such as streptomycin. He estimated that it would take six months and $1 million to convert the existing facilities for this use.

Unfortunately, renovation work at the Vigo plant started out as a perfect example of Murphy's Law, as one delay followed another. Continual breakdowns in power supply — erratic electricity, broken

steam lines, malfunctioning compressors, and pump failures — all contributed to the contamination of huge batches of streptomycin. By 1949, however, the difficulties with infrastructure had been resolved, and Vigo was producing sufficient streptomycin to keep up with growing demand. Streptomycin fermentation was on course.

Despite this progress, Pfizer knew it could not afford to become complacent. The company's scientists continued their quest to find new antibiotics to fight disease. Pfizer's first antibiotic, penicillin, had arrived in Alexander Fleming's lab literally out of thin air. The next germ killer might be anywhere on Earth — or more likely, somewhere in the earth itself. So Pfizer began a soil-screening program in search of antibiotics.

The company launched a worldwide soil collection and testing program. Pfizer solicited and received 135,000 soil samples on which its scientists conducted more than 20 million tests. In the words of Pfizer microbiologist Ben Sobin:

A 1949 photograph shows the giant recovery tanks in the Brooklyn Works that were used to recover streptomycin from the broth.

A group of Pfizer officers in 1948. John L. Smith and John Powers, Sr., are seated in the front row, first and third from left. In the back row, John McKeen is at the far left. John Powers, Sr., retired as vice president of sales in 1945 but remained a director until 1949.

We got soil samples from cemeteries; we had balloons up in the air collecting soil samples that were wind borne; we got soil from the bottoms of mine shafts; we got soil from the bottom of the ocean; we got soil from the desert; we got it from the tops of mountains and the bottoms of mountains and in between.

Pfizer scientists suspended each soil sample in water, then placed it on culture plates to incubate. Any mold colonies that looked promising were applied to a series of harmful bacteria. If the mold killed the bacteria, the researchers isolated and cultivated it. As soon as they established that a particular mold had antibiotic properties, they scaled up production to cultivate these properties. Eventually, the scientists identified 200 new antibiotic-containing molds.

It was an exciting time at Pfizer. As the midpoint of the 20th century neared, a new generation of leaders took the helm. John McKeen became president, George Anderson retired, and despite a serious medical condition, John L. Smith took his place as chairman of the board. That same year, Pfizer celebrated its 100th anniversary. Poised on the edge of a new decade, with a daring new leader, the company was about to set off on a course of double-digit growth that would send Pfizer and its products to every corner of the world.

This 1950 photo illustrates the rigorous testing of penicillin samples in Pfizer's Quality Control Department.

CHAPTER NINE

CONQUERING NEW FRONTIERS

THE 1950S

If anything comes out of this antibiotic soil-screening program, don't make the mistake we made with penicillin and hand it over to other companies. Let's sell it ourselves. Go into the pharmaceutical business if we have to.

— John L. Smith, 1950

AS SOIL SAMPLES POURED in, Pfizer's researchers tested some 5,000 cultures a month. Following the introduction of paper chromatography, which separated complex mixtures into zones of pure substances, the team could better analyze the chemical elements that they found in soil samples.

Finally, in late 1949, Pfizer hit "pay dirt" with a substance found in soil taken from the Midwestern United States that proved effective against a wide range of deadly bacteria. Its code name, PA-76, identified it as the 76th culture of a "Pfizer Antibiotic." This product — the first developed exclusively by Pfizer's own scientists — was named Terramycin. According to John McKeen, the name was appropriate: "I wanted a name connected with the earth, and one that could easily be recalled by doctors and scientists and people in general, because it came from the earth."

At first, PA-76 was so close to Aureomycin on the chromatography assay that some Pfizer staff mistook it for that antibiotic. But Jasper Kane found the crucial differences that led Pfizer's team to conclude that it had discovered an even more powerful antibiotic. Years later, he vividly recalled his first sight of Terramycin at work: "I used to walk in every morning and examine the chromatographic strips that were seeded the night before.

But one morning there was a great big empty space where some antibiotic had killed all the bacteria in that area."

Sensing the enormity of this discovery, Pfizer immediately brought scientists in from different disciplines to study PA-76. Gladys Hobby, a member of the original penicillin team, and pharmacologist S.Y. P'an were put in charge of testing the new compound. The crash program swung into high gear. Compared to the huge effort that had gone into the steep penicillin/streptomycin learning curve, PA-76 evolved from dirt to drug with lightning speed. In only a few months, Pfizer refined production techniques, filed for patent protection, and completed rigorous clinical testing.

On New Year's Eve in 1950, Gladys Hobby conducted Terramycin's first human trial at New York's Harlem Hospital. The results of the tests surpassed Pfizer's highest expectations. Patients' fevers plunged, infections were cured, and side effects were minimal. Pfizer executives were immediately informed of the encouraging results. Although

Pfizer's soil-screening program, started in 1945, brought in more than 135,000 samples like those pictured above and four years later led to the discovery of Terramycin, a broad-spectrum antibiotic.

hospitalized with cancer himself, Smith was particularly thrilled to hear the news of Pfizer's latest breakthrough.

From his deathbed, he advised his successor, John McKeen, "If anything comes of this antibiotic soil-screening program, don't make the mistake we made with penicillin and hand it over to other companies. Let's sell it ourselves. Go into the pharmaceutical business if we have to."

The Pfizer Label

Smith's advice was sound, but easier said than done. Selling directly to hospitals and pharmacies would bring Pfizer head to head with many long-term customers — drug companies that had relied on the Brooklyn plant for raw materials as well as finished products. Building a domestic pharmaceutical sales force would transform Pfizer as profoundly as its shift to research had. Moreover, fail-

ure might strip the company of all its customers, both old and new.

When Pfizer's management met in the same room at the Brooklyn plant where they had voted to try to mass-produce penicillin, the lesson of their recent past was clear. Pfizer had pioneered penicillin production while other companies walked away with the lion's share of the profits. With a new breakthrough in hand, the company had the opportunity to bring Terramycin to the world under its own label. The Pfizer team knew

Left: A greatly magnified tetracycline crystal.

Below: Four years after Terramycin, Pfizer introduced Tetracyn (tetracycline), the first purely synthesized broad-spectrum antibiotic discovered by Pfizer. Here, Lloyd Conover, second from left, whose name is on the U.S. patent, meets with the chemists on his research team, from left, James Korst, David Johnston, and Kenneth Butler.

Above: The original Terramycin team formed the backbone of Pfizer's Antibiotic Research Division. First row from left: Don Seeley, John B. Routien, Gladys Hobby, Ben A. Sobin, and Jasper Kane. Back row from left: J.W. Vinson, Tom Lees, I.A. Solomons, Peter Regna, and S.Y. P'an. Team members Al Finlay and Gil Shull are not pictured.

Left: The original Terramycin patent issued in 1950. The list of discoverers includes Pfizer scientists Ben Sobin, Al Finlay, and Jasper Kane. Terramycin was the company's first branded drug.

there was only one option: to honor Smith's wishes and once again put everything on the line.

As expected, the company's decision provoked howls of protest from pharmaceutical and chemical customers alike. Pfizer's chemical salesmen were deluged with angry phone calls, and one pharmaceutical firm declared that it would buy products from any company but Pfizer. McKeen, however, would not budge. "What we lose in the old chemical business," he said, "we'll make up in the new business. And more."

Above: Nobel laureate Robert B. Woodward of Harvard University, left, is shown discussing the Terramycin molecule with Pfizer scientists F.A. Hochstein, center, and Karl J. Brunings.

Below: To test new antibiotics, scientists placed discs treated with medicine on a petri dish that had been seeded with germs, a technique similar to that used by Fleming. Efficacy was determined by a dark "kill zone" around the antibiotic.

He was right. Pfizer's new antibiotic was a record-breaking success. Tragically, John L. Smith, the man who had done so much to position Pfizer for its debut as a full-fledged pharmaceutical company, did not live to savor his triumph. On July 10, 1950, barely four months after the launch of Terramycin, he succumbed to cancer. Pfizer lost a heroic leader, but the Terramycin launch was a splendid tribute to the man under whose direction Pfizer scientists had perfected citric acid fermentation and the mass production of antibiotics.

Tributes to Smith poured in from major newspapers around the world. The trade publication *Oil, Paint & Drug Reporter* expressed the views of many when it wrote:

The crowning achievement of Mr. Smith's career was unquestionably the role he played in the development of the first great antibiotic, penicillin, which has led to opening the

whole field of antibiotic research and development which means so much to the public health of all nations.

Pfizer Goes Global

John Smith's passing marked the end of an era. After building a successful pharmaceutical business, Pfizer was poised to become a global enterprise. Three visionaries would lead that huge undertaking: Pfizer President John McKeen; his assistant, Jack Powers; and Don Hilton, who had been hired in 1947 as Pfizer's first international sales manager. These men looked across the oceans and saw that the need for effective medicines had never been greater. They recognized that Europe and Asia were still recovering from the war and that people in developing nations were clamoring for a better way of life. Pfizer's leaders realized that they stood on the threshold of an unprecedented era of global growth.

In 1950, Jack Powers pointed out to McKeen that Pfizer's competitors were reaping big profits overseas. Both men recognized that Terramycin gave Pfizer an historic opportunity to break into international markets. Powers asked McKeen: "Who will take Pfizer around the world?" Without hesitation, McKeen replied, "You do it!"

Jack Powers was ready to lead the charge. Starting with a network of sales agents in a few countries, Pfizer began establishing offices, subsidiaries, and partnerships around the world. Despite senior management's great enthusiasm, the company's inexperience soon hampered its progress. Jack Powers set off on a global fact-finding mission — only to discover that the agents themselves were the basic problem.

As Powers later recounted:

They made a lot of money on Pfizer, and it was really tough to change from agents to our own branches, as we called them then. But the one agent that really got me going was a man from Cuba. He came in for lunch and we were talking. He pulled out a wallet and showed me some pictures. I said, "Oh, isn't this nice? Is this your country club?"

"No, no," he said, "that's my home in Havana. Of course, I have another one outside the city, in the country." I'll never forget the impact of that. Here was this guy making a fortune out of Pfizer and we had done all the scientific work. I made up my mind then, we were going to take over from all these agents.

At a long Saturday meeting in 1951, Powers outlined his game plan for Pfizer's International Division. He challenged his team to put the company on the map. Setting an annual goal of $60 million in international sales, Powers announced that the time had come to "go global." He urged his sales people to "study the economy, establish proper contacts with government officials, learn the language, history, and customs, and hire local employees wherever possible."

Initially, Powers and Hilton focused on opening Pfizer offices in Canada, Cuba, Mexico, England, and Belgium. By late 1951, Pfizer Canada, Ltd., was fully operational, with a Montreal facility to package and distribute antibiotics under Pfizer's label. Pfizer Canada, Ltd., was quickly followed by Laboratorios Pfizer, S.A., with offices in Mexico City, Puerto Rico, Brazil, Panama, and Cuba. In Belgium, Pfizer International Corporation, in partnership with a local company, packaged and distributed drugs for Europe and the Middle East. The following September, Pfizer acquired the Fursland Laboratories in Brazil.

Powers coupled these overseas sales offices with new manufacturing plants. His idea was to seize the competitive advantage by eliminating tariffs and taxes that would have been levied on imported products. With local plants, Pfizer could also cater to regional tastes, such as the French and Italian preference for injectibles over oral medication and the German preference for lemon-flavored medicinals.

By March 1953, the company had three new manufacturing companies overseas: Pfizer, Ltd., in England, Pfizer Belgium, and Pfizer Inter-American S.A. in Panama. With operations in Belgium and England and a distribution network in South America and the Far East, Pfizer was poised to become a global powerhouse. As the company continued to raise its flag in new nations, it divided the world into four regions: Europe, the Western Hemisphere, the Far East, and the Middle East. In theory, each area would be run by a regional director from headquarters in Manhattan. In practice, Pfizer gave its people tremendous autonomy to develop new opportunities, make critical decisions, and execute them on the spot.

A typical Pfizer overseas operation ran on a shoestring budget from a single cramped office with a handful of employees. The only American was usually the country manager, who reported to an area manager, who in turn reported directly to Jack Powers. With each new year, the global

Shown arriving in Chile in 1962, John Powers, Jr., is flanked by two of the top men in Pfizer International. On the left is Bill Deckert, responsible for South America; on the right is Bob Middlebrook, in charge of Asia. Powers established Pfizer's International Division.

gamble proved to be a winning bet. By 1959, Pfizer had achieved stunning success — generating nearly 85 percent of its profits from international operations. The company gained even greater momentum when it plowed the lion's share of those revenues back into the local operations that had produced them.

Reinvestment was central to Powers' philosophy: "We want to dig our foundations deep and grow," he said. "This is the way to contribute to a country's progress and to Pfizer's." Powers never forgot those days. As he later remarked, "We were unencumbered by experience, so we didn't realize the problems. There was nobody to tell us, 'You can't do it.' Taking chances and gambles made it a joyous time."

Terramycin in Demand

Thanks to Terramycin, it was also an exceptional time for sales and profits — both in the United States and abroad. In the first years of Terramycin's production, between 1950 and 1952, booming demand for the new drug triggered record growth. Sales of Terramycin doubled company rev-

Above: Detailers, as sales reps were called, traveled the world spreading the message about Pfizer pharmaceuticals. Here, a sales rep discusses Pfizer products at the Hospital Provincial de Madrid in Spain.

Right: Terramycin propelled the growth of Pfizer's animal health products in the 1950s. Here, a veterinarian prepares to administer Terramycin on a farm in Venezuela.

enues to $107 million. By 1953, Pfizer had hired some 1,300 "detail men" — the term for drug representatives in the trade — to promote the company's new wonder drug. Terramycin was so popular that the salesmen spent their first months on the job simply taking orders.

The drug's effectiveness and adaptability helped spur its tremendous success. Originally sold as a capsule, it was later available in a variety of forms. New applications were also constantly being developed. In 1952 alone, Pfizer introduced 15 new variations of Terramycin, including a flavored oral formula and a broad array of dosages in every conceivable strength. Terramycin was even proven effective for livestock and agricultural applications. Such extraordinary versatility assured its place as one of the industry's best-selling products.

From the beginning of the penicillin boom, leaders like Smith and McKeen saw antibiotics as the key to Pfizer's future growth. In 1952, Pfizer established a separate Antibiotics Division, with sections for research, marketing, and manufacturing — all led by Ernst Weber, executive director of Biomedical Research, and Jasper Kane, vice president of Scientific Affairs. Meanwhile, Groton became the largest fermentation plant in the world as Pfizer steadily transferred Terramycin production from Brooklyn to Connecticut.

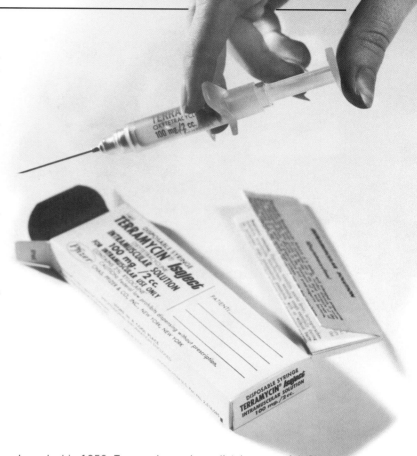

Launched in 1950, Terramycin was immediately successful. Shown here is its formulation for injection, introduced in the early 1960s.

Animal Health Takes Shape

From their early investigations, Pfizer's researchers were convinced that Terramycin would benefit animals as well. They observed that those given antibiotic-fortified feed grew faster and were healthier than those fed the standard diet. In 1950, Pfizer introduced Bi-Con, its first animal health product, which combined vitamin B-12 and streptomycin fermentation residue.

The scientists' research quickly convinced them that Terramycin would be far more effective in preserving animal health than streptomycin. They even devised a formula to save piglets. At the time, about one third of the pigs born in the United States died each year because sows tended to roll over and crush their nursing offspring.

If Pfizer could develop a safe formula to feed the piglets, millions could be saved. Pfizer animal nutritionist Herb Luther set out to meet this challenge, working on the super-secret "Project Piglet." He was so obsessed with security that he set up shop in a deserted SUCIAC laboratory in Building 3B in Brooklyn and paid for all materials — bottles, nipples, and cages — out of his own pocket.

Luther's team showed great ingenuity in dealing with the piglets. To bottle-feed them, the scientists built a special trough with nipples. To replicate the piglets' normal cycle of sleeping, waking, and feeding, the researchers used music to "set the mood" — awakening them with the "William Tell Overture" and lulling them to sleep with "Brahms' Lullaby."

Luther's team named the formula that they developed Terralac and tested it at R&L Farms in Shoemakersville, Pennsylvania. Initial results were outstanding. Adding the antibiotic to feed for live-

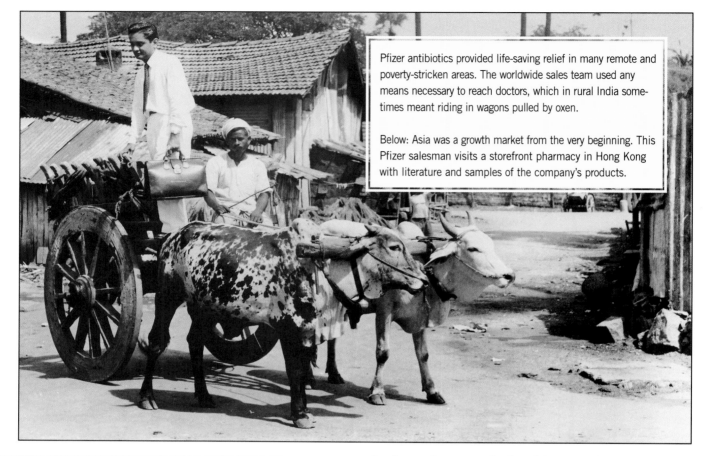

Pfizer antibiotics provided life-saving relief in many remote and poverty-stricken areas. The worldwide sales team used any means necessary to reach doctors, which in rural India sometimes meant riding in wagons pulled by oxen.

Below: Asia was a growth market from the very beginning. This Pfizer salesman visits a storefront pharmacy in Hong Kong with literature and samples of the company's products.

stock made animals healthier and saved grain. Luther presented the formula to the Sales Division for distribution. McKeen saw the potential of veterinary and agricultural research and pushed to expand it.

Pfizer's Agricultural Research and Development Center was born in 1952 when the company built a 700-acre farm and research center at the Vigo plant in Terre Haute. In recognition of what Luther had achieved, he was appointed director of research and development at Vigo in 1953. Later, the plant would expand into a 45-acre experimental farm for animal nutrition and veterinary medicine, complete with state-of-the-art equipment.

Between 1953 and 1955, the Agricultural Division introduced a variety of products, including Agrimycin, which combined both streptomycin and Terramycin. By the end of the decade, animal products that targeted fever in cattle and leptospirosis in swine measurably boosted growth rates.

As Pfizer forged new trails at home and abroad, John McKeen became not only the influential leader of a pacesetting company respected in the pharmaceutical industry, but also a popular advocate for the industry itself. McKeen frequently spoke (and was a published writer) on trends in pharmaceutical development and on the industry's contributions to society. He traveled extensively, speaking to organizations that ranged from local chambers of commerce, regional business groups, and civic forums to the New York Society of Security Analysts. McKeen also campaigned tirelessly on college campuses, encouraging students to set their sights on careers in his industry.

Thanks to McKeen's efforts, Pfizer's breakthrough antibiotics, and its creativity in marketing and sales, the company soon became well known. Numerous national publications recorded Pfizer's medical exploits in laudatory features.

In 1952, a 700-acre Agricultural Research and Development Center was established at Pfizer's Vigo plant in Terre Haute, Indiana.

Hardly a week went by without news of John McKeen's gift of Terramycin to a world figure or the company's being acclaimed "one of the wonders" of the fast-growing wonder-drug industry.

When a reporter for *The New Yorker* went to the Brooklyn Works to do a story on antibiotic research, McKeen told him that antibiotics were "life-saving miracles," adding, "When you can make a living by helping somebody else in the world, you've got a pretty good life."

To increase the company's name recognition with future doctors, Pfizer hired 70 medical students in 1951 to work for the company during their summer break. They received a brief, intensive orientation in the use of antibiotics, then dispersed to 40 cities across the country to educate local medical personnel on the proper use of Terramycin and other Pfizer products.

The company also produced a newsletter for doctors, dentists, nurses, and veterinarians that focused on recent findings in the field of antibiotics. The newsletter won both kudos and credi-

I think to a large extent it was inevitable. The phar-maceutical companies were considered the makers of miracle drugs, which put us all in the limelight, and then Sen. Estes Kefauver came along and put us in a bad light.

The Federal Trade Commission (FTC) had been quietly studying pharmaceutical companies for years. Its report noted that 29 new antibiotics had been put on the market between 1949 and 1956. The FTC charged that American Cyanamid and Pfizer controlled almost 38 percent of the entire market for antibiotics and that "certain patents have been handled in ways that [might] represent a conflict with the antitrust laws." The Federal Trade Commission further accused six companies, includ-

Left: Working under sterile conditions, an employee monitors a Terramycin packaging machine as it fills glass ampules.

Below: An employee carefully inspects Terramycin ampules, part of Pfizer's rigorous quality control procedure, at the company's Toluca, Mexico, plant in 1962.

bility for covering the successes of Pfizer's competitors, as well as the occasional setbacks in its own research and development.

In 1959, the company arranged to have *The New York Times* place Pfizer's Annual Report as a Sunday supplement. The piece generated so much favorable publicity that *Industrial Marketing* proclaimed Pfizer "Company of the Year" for its innovative approach to public relations.

The Tide Turns

Although the 1950s had begun for Pfizer in the bright sunshine of new cures, they ended under a dark cloud. As the decade drew to a close, the U.S. government charged a substantial number of pharmaceutical companies with price fixing and collusion.

Jack Powers could not refrain from noting the irony behind the charges:

This was a bitter blow, because if there's ever been fierce competition, it was in the field of broad-spectrum antibiotics. We had killed each other. But

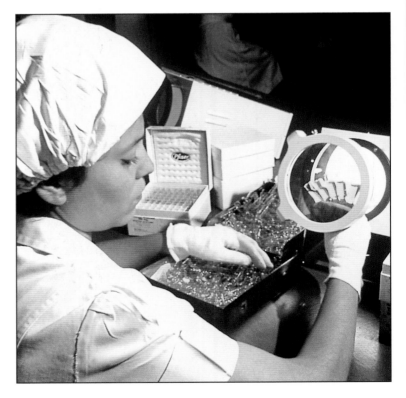

ing Pfizer, of fixing prices. The charges ran the gamut from alleged attempts to monopolize tetracycline and its derivatives to conspiracy to obtain fraudulent patents on these drugs.

John McKeen responded with a categorical denial: "Pfizer has never engaged in a conspiracy, never misused its patents, never fixed prices, and wields no monopolistic powers. The charges that Pfizer misled the Patent Office and withheld information are utterly baseless."

The patent in dispute was for tetracycline, which had sparked inter-industry warfare several years earlier. Pfizer's main product was Terramycin (oxytetracycline), and its chief competitor was Aureomycin (chlortetracycline). The strength of these two powerful antibiotics motivated pharmaceutical companies to delve into tetracycline's chemistry. Pfizer felt confident that if the Aureomycin molecule could be stripped clean of its chlorine atom, it had potential as a stand-alone antibiotic.

The company succeeded in its quest and applied for a patent for its newly named antibiotic, Tetracyn. Pfizer, however, was not alone in its race to isolate the tetracycline molecule. Scientists at the Lederle Company had also succeeded in extracting the tetracycline molecule from Aureomycin. Five months after Pfizer's patent application, American Cyanamid, the parent company of Lederle, applied for its own patent under the name of Achromycin.

When both companies received a notice of interference from the U.S. Patent Office, they negotiated a settlement. Pfizer gained priority on its

Above: The Accounting Department in Brooklyn, shown in a photograph taken in the 1950s, swelled as the company reaped the rewards of Terramycin. Pfizer's worldwide organization expanded rapidly.

Below: To celebrate its 110th anniversary, the company arranged to have its annual report inserted in *The New York Times* as a Sunday supplement. The report generated much favorable publicity.

tetracycline patent application and received a non-exclusive right to manufacture Aureomycin, which was necessary for the manufacture of tetracycline. In exchange, American Cyanamid received the nonexclusive right to manufacture tetracycline. Since it filed its application first, Pfizer received the tetracycline patent.

The truce did not last because as soon as the chemical makeup of tetracycline was published, a third company, Bristol Laboratories, claimed that it had been manufacturing tetracycline all along. Bristol filed its own application for a patent in October 1953, a year after Pfizer. The upshot was yet another declaration of interference.

In October 1954, patent examiner H.J. Lidoff halted the interference proceedings on tetracycline hydrochloride and announced that tetracycline itself was not patentable because it was a byproduct of Aureomycin production. After Pfizer proved that this was not the case, the company was once again declared the patent holder of the drug in January 1955. Although Pfizer promptly filed infringement suits against the other companies selling tetracycline, all three were eventually granted a nonexclusive right to manufacture and sell it.

Although this arrangement was satisfactory to the companies, it was interpreted as an illegal conspiracy in the FTC report. Once the report was published, major newspapers across the country ran the story. For the first time, pharmaceutical companies felt the heat of public disapproval. The FTC formally filed charges of conspiracy and monopolization against Pfizer, American Cyanamid, Bristol, Squibb, and Upjohn. Hearings were scheduled for January 1959.

The FTC charges provided a perfect platform for Estes Kefauver, a senator from Tennessee with White House ambitions. As chairman of the Senate Judiciary Subcommittee on Antitrust and Monopoly, Kefauver took direct aim at the pharmaceutical industry and sponsored a hearing to explore drug research, testing, costs, and pricing.

Kefauver grabbed headlines by charging that drugs, which sometimes consisted of raw materials worth mere pennies, were often marked up 1,000 percent — or more. The pharmaceutical manufacturers fought back with a comprehensive campaign to educate the public about the expenses incurred in discovering and developing drugs. Then Kefauver launched a second attack, focusing the hearings on the allegedly fatal side effects of Diabinese, Pfizer's popular oral antidiabetic drug.

Although the charges were proven to be false, Pfizer took extraordinary steps to protect the integrity of Diabinese. The medicine signaled a new direction for the company. As its first once-a-day drug and the first major non-antibiotic, or non-fermentation, product, it had rapidly become a bestseller.

McKeen approached every hearing like a man on a mission. Armed with exhaustive documentation, detailed case studies, corroborative findings from independent scientists at universities, and related discoveries by researchers at rival companies, he gave the subcommittee a crash course in all aspects of Diabinese's development.

Pfizer's leader was completely forthcoming about every aspect of the drug's cost and pricing. He enlightened the committee with cost breakdowns of various Pfizer research projects, even citing examples of extensive, costly research and testing that had failed to lead to a viable drug. McKeen went everywhere, monitored every proceeding, and refuted any statement he considered inaccurate. He even went so far as to rebut Kefauver's statements and to distribute his own — even before the Senator's press releases had gone out.

McKeen, Pfizer's one-man dynamo, along with the company's scientists and other executives, had done their homework. As the hearings continued, it became clear that legislation to impose price controls was going nowhere. When the subcommittee reconvened after a summer recess, Senator Kefauver's combative tone had disappeared, and he praised Pfizer, noting that the company's prices for penicillin were nearly 50 percent less than those of its competitors.

Although the battle ended in victory, the war would continue. After nearly three years of exhaustive hearings, which included witnesses, documents, and a full trial, FTC hearing examiner Robert Piper threw out all charges of price fixing against Pfizer, American Cyanamid, Upjohn, Bristol-Myers Company, Bristol Laboratories (a subsidiary of Bristol-Myers Company), and Olin Mathieson. The Department of Justice, however, examined the same 11,000 pages of evidence

Bill Steere's 1959 training class gathered for this photograph in the company's New York City headquarters. Steere is shown in the middle.

and filed its own criminal complaint against Pfizer, Bristol, and American Cyanamid for conspiring to restrict competition and fix prices. Criminal charges were also filed personally against John McKeen.

Once again, Pfizer mobilized its resources and mounted a spirited defense. The Federal Court dismissed the charges against McKeen in 1965, but the charges against Pfizer and the other companies had serious repercussions. They helped usher in a new era of government oversight in the production of drugs, and they prompted a broad diversification of Pfizer's product lineup. As Jack Powers remarked in 1991:

It was not only a question of being sensitive to the law and taking counsel carefully, but also [of] being sensitive to government regulations and practice. We learned that men like Kefauver can take some subject matter and run with it for their own purposes. And they can do considerable damage to your company. Therefore, you need to understand the system. We have had an office in Washington since those days.

In 1959, when the company was facing one of the most difficult challenges in its history, Pfizer hired a man who would — three decades later — lead Pfizer to unprecedented success. Fresh out of Stanford University with a B.A. in marine biology, William C. Steere, Jr., joined Pfizer as a medical sales representative. He immediately caught the attention of Pfizer management when he turned his first territory, California's San Joaquin Valley, into one of the region's top-producing areas. When he became CEO in 1991 and chairman of the board in 1992, Steere would help make Pfizer one of the world's leading pharmaceutical companies.

By the close of the 1950s, Pfizer had achieved the goals it had set at the start of the decade. The company had successfully transformed itself from a supplier into a pharmaceutical enterprise selling products under its own label. It had also established plants and/or sales representatives in every region of the world. To take the next step and become the acknowledged global leader in the industry, Pfizer would have to meet the challenge of building a research division that would be second to none.

In 1961, Pfizer established its world headquarters in this skyscraper in the heart of Manhattan.

CHAPTER TEN

PFIZER IN TRANSITION

1960–1969

As the leadership of the company passed from John McKeen to John Powers, there was a very important intellectual transition. The two men were as different as day and night. They complemented each other beautifully during the McKeen era because McKeen was a go-get-'em, activist kind of guy. He dealt with everybody face to face. Powers was much more of an intellectual, more interested in the theoretical elements of management.

— Barry Bloom

THROUGHOUT THE 1960s, Pfizer built on its tradition of innovation and excellence, continuing to raise its profile around the world. The decade began with the opening of two new sites: a corporate headquarters building at 235 East 42nd Street in the heart of Manhattan and a new research center in Groton, Connecticut. To underline the symbolic importance of the new building in Manhattan, the board of directors officially moved the company's headquarters from Brooklyn to Manhattan, where Pfizer has been based ever since.

Groton

In 1960, Pfizer management and employees celebrated the grand opening of the Medical Research Laboratories in Groton. The 177,000-square-foot research facility would conduct a fully integrated research program against a variety of medical problems, including heart and blood vessel ailments, arthritis, mental illness, infectious diseases, and metabolic disorders. Set on 19 wooded acres across the road from Pfizer's fermentation plant, the Groton research site featured a massive bronze statue of Hermes, the messenger of the Greek gods as well as the patron of commerce and innovation.

Despite improved research facilities, the mood inside Pfizer's young research organization was somber. The team struggled with a crisis of confidence. Ogden Tanner, author of *Twenty-Five Years of Innovation: The Story of Pfizer Central Research*, observed, "The late 1950s and early 1960s were a period of uncertainty and stagnation. The research group seemed to be marking time." Since the introduction of Terramycin, a decade had slipped by with no major success other than Diabinese, which had come under fire in the Kefauver hearings.

Pfizer scientists at the time were like brilliant actors in need of a good director. Most of the biological research was carried out at the company's site in Maywood, New Jersey, later named the John L. Smith Cancer Research Center. Medicinal chemistry scientists were in the Brooklyn labs, while other Pfizer scientists worked in Sandwich, England, and in the Vigo plant in Terre Haute, Indiana. Although the Research Division enjoyed robust growth, with hundreds of scientists joining the staff and the research budget swelling from $10 million to $250 million during the 1950s, that growth was generally unfocused.

This bronze statue of the Greek god Hermes, patron of commerce and innovation, was placed in front of the new Medical Research Laboratories in Groton, Connecticut, when they opened in 1960.

Above: In the early 1960s, Gladys Hobby, left, and John Davenport, right, visited Pfizer's Maywood facility in New Jersey, which was later converted into the John L. Smith Cancer Research Center.

Below: In 1960, Groton became the headquarters of Pfizer's research operations with the opening of the Medical Research Laboratories.

Edward Wiseman, executive director of Research Administration, who started his Pfizer career at the company's Sandwich, England, facility and would later become the chief biologist for Pfizer's future blockbuster drug, Feldene, explains why the industry lacked focus:

There was no real pharmaceutical industry until the post-fifties. In the fifties, you had an enormous number of chemicals that were made during the war to replace chemicals reserved for the war effort. But they were not pharmaceuticals. They were dye stuffs, gunpowders, ersatz coffee, everything. So the pharmaceutical industry in the fifties was based on gathering all of those chemicals, testing them and hoping something would happen.

In the sixties, a lot of people began thinking about biological mechanisms. Everybody began realizing that there must be something inside us that goes wrong when we're sick. And they began looking for receptor sites — why when you swallow a pill, the chemical knows where to go. It knows to cure your headache and not go down to your feet, where it won't do any good. Most people realized that there must be an assemblage of proteins somewhere, and people dreamed about where these might be.

Pfizer's expanding research efforts enabled new scientific fields to blossom at the company. One of these, organic chemistry, contrasted sharply

John McKeen was determined to direct the company's growth. In 1960, he and John Powers, left, announced the "5-by-5" sales goal of $500 million by 1965. It was achieved in December 1965.

with microbiology, Pfizer's traditional strong suit. Whereas a microbiologist produces fermentation products and then tests their biological activity, an organic chemist synthesizes new molecules to specifically attack a target disease at the cellular level.

As Pfizer's researchers explored new possibilities, the company continued to perform well, thanks to a strong portfolio of antibiotics and rising chemical sales. Overseas, Terramycin was a power brand, selling briskly in both injectable and oral forms. Also gaining acceptance were Antivert, for severe headaches and dizziness, the antidepressant Niamid, the medium-spectrum antibiotic Tao, and the broad-spectrum antibiotics Sigmamycin and Tetracyn. In 1960, the company also introduced a new synthetic penicillin and reported advances in vaccines for measles, croup, and infant bronchitis.

Determined that Pfizer's growth would develop according to a plan, John McKeen steered the entire company toward an ambitious goal — "5-by-5" — $500 million in sales by 1965. Despite the distrac-

tion and distress caused by the Kefauver hearings, Pfizer not only met but surpassed this goal. When McKeen announced the good news, he predicted that the figure, huge as it then seemed, would be only a fraction of what the company would achieve.

Although Pfizer had successfully defended its position during the Kefauver hearings, those proceedings eventually led to legislation that profoundly and permanently changed the entire pharmaceutical industry: the Kefauver-Harris Amendments to the Food, Drug, and Cosmetic Act. This legislation completely transformed the process for securing drug approvals. Before the amendments, pharmaceutical companies had usually gained approval for pending drugs within months of applying.

In this 1960s photo, a sales representative in Japan is en route to his next appointment. Pfizer's presence in what is today the world's second largest pharmaceutical market began in the mid-1950s as a joint venture. In 1995, Pfizer Seiyaku, now a wholly owned subsidiary, became Pfizer's first international unit to exceed $1 billion in sales.

After the amendments, the Food and Drug Administration (FDA) acquired the power to increase its regulation of the industry, oversee the development of new drugs, and require long and comprehensive trials. The new regulations, along with scientific advances that added more levels of complexity to the drug-development process, dramatically raised the cost of research and slowed down the entire process. Now, the time required to carry out research and gain approval began to consume an increasing percentage of the 17 years allotted patents, which started from the time of application. As a consequence, it became much harder to market drugs successfully and to generate the capital necessary to plow back into research.

Branching Out

In response, McKeen plotted a course that would decrease Pfizer's dependence on pharmaceuticals. Between 1957 and 1964, the company acquired nearly 30 different businesses. These acquisitions, in John McKeen's words, opened new fields of "exploration and development" and provided a diverse line of "products that [would] appeal to two billion people in the free world." Explaining the rationale for the company's diversification, *Time* magazine noted that "by creating and developing products that were all, in some way, involved with chemistry, Pfizer gets maximum yield from its seemingly disparate acquisitions."

The acquisitions spanned the landscape of industrial America: Some were original suppliers to Pfizer; others manufactured products that gave the company access to markets it had never penetrated before. For example, Pfizer's acquisition of Morningstar-Paisley eased the company's entry into such areas as flexible packaging, paper, food, textiles, oil, and mining. Leeming and Pacquin, manufacturers of proprietary drugs and toiletries, provided an established relationship with supermarkets, and the purchase of the Coty cosmetic line put Pfizer into an entirely new business, further broadening its distribution channels.

In the marketplace, Pfizer seemed to move effortlessly from one success to another. On the legal front, however, it remained in a quagmire. A costly new battle forced Pfizer to fight in the courtroom against injustice just as it had fought in the laboratory against disease. In October 1967, Pfizer and codefendants Bristol, American Cyanamid, Upjohn, and Squibb had to defend themselves against charges of attempting to monopolize the tetracycline market.

On December 29, the jury returned a verdict of guilty. Each of the three companies was fined $150,000. The fines themselves were manageable, but the verdict opened the door to a flood of additional lawsuits. About 150 were filed, seeking damages on behalf of rival companies, consumers, hospitals, health care consortiums, and wholesale and retail sellers worldwide. Jack Powers, the CEO, commented, "I remember calling the lawyers one time and saying, 'Just tell me what we're talking about as a potential for damages to Pfizer itself.' Well, they studied the subject, came back, and said it would be about $2.5 billion. I was flabbergasted."

The companies believed the decision would be overturned but nevertheless opted to settle the

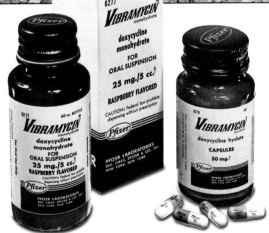

pending lawsuits. They offered $100 million to "government entities and hospitals in the United States, retailers, wholesalers, and consumers," and the final amount approved was $82 million.

Although the civil antitrust damage settlements were upheld, the U.S. Court of Appeals in New York reversed the 1967 criminal conviction that had prompted them. The Justice Department immediately petitioned the U.S. Supreme Court, seeking a reconsideration of the appellate decision. In 1972, the Supreme Court upheld the appellate decision and cleared Pfizer of price fixing.

Twenty-five years after Pfizer had received its tetracycline patent and eight years after the patent had actually expired, Philadelphia Federal Judge Charles Weiner formally cleared Pfizer of the Federal Trade Commission's charges that the company had fraudulently obtained its patent for tetracycline.

Above: Vibramycin, introduced in 1967, was the company's first once-a-day broad-spectrum antibiotic and quickly became a top seller.

Top: A group photo of a Vibramycin sales team. Third from right, front row, is George Stone, who headed the team.

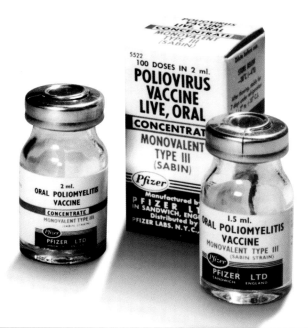

Pfizer Fights Polio

Despite such frustrations, Pfizer never lost sight of its mission: to win the war against disease. Just as Pfizer had risen to the occasion in the Second World War by discovering how to mass-produce penicillin, in the next decade it joined the battle against polio, a terrifying scourge at home.

In the 1950s, polio was the most feared childhood disease. It spread during hot summer months when children crowded around public swimming pools. Polio attacked and destroyed the nerve cells that control muscular movement, often leaving its victims permanently paralyzed. When polio attacked nerve cells in the respiratory system, the result could be even worse, condemning the patient to a lifetime in an "iron lung."

Polio was a parent's nightmare, so when vaccines became available, thousands of parents brought their children to vaccination centers on Sabin Oral Sundays for their dose of protection.

Above: The live-virus polio vaccine developed by Dr. Albert Sabin was a key weapon in the effort to eradicate polio in the U.S.

and civic groups together to immunize more than 50 million men, women, and children in a mighty effort to eradicate this dread disease.

Scene, the company's employee magazine, expressed pride in Pfizer's accomplishment: "By enlisting the support of entire communities, from pharmacist to physician and from boy scout to banker, Pfizer has helped bring the eradication of polio well within sight."

Streamlining Research

Despite the company's success with the polio vaccine, the Research Division was languishing. In 1963, McKeen decided it was time to shake up research. He asked his most trusted lieutenant, Jack Powers, to turn his attention from the overseas business to streamlining the division's various departments. Powers agreed and promptly immersed himself in Pfizer research. He quickly realized that having labs spread across every discipline and around the globe was not conducive to a focused research effort. Powers also recognized that organic chemists, microbiologists, pharmacologists, and other scientists were working in isolation. Moreover, rivalries often flared among the groups. Too often, scientific discovery in materials, agriculture, or consumer goods was conducted independently, with

Pfizer made development of a polio vaccine an imperative and played a key role in producing and distributing Dr. Jonas Salk's killed-virus immunization. The Pfizer facility in Sandwich, England, started bulk production in 1958, with $2.5 million invested in the development of the Salk vaccine.

Meanwhile, in Cincinnati, Dr. Albert Sabin, assisted by a Pfizer grant, had formulated his own "live-virus" polio vaccine. Pfizer won the sole right to market the Type I Sabin Oral vaccine. The drug was a huge success. Children quickly discovered that eating vaccine-laden sugar cubes was far more pleasant than undergoing injections.

Working with local health services, company representatives fanned out across America. Pfizer helped organize mass-immunization programs to administer Type I of the Sabin Oral vaccine. This effort, promoted as S.O.S. — Sabin Oral Sundays — brought doctors, nurses, pharmacists, parents,

Above: When Dr. Albert Sabin, left, announced that he was developing a live-virus vaccine for polio, Pfizer's chairman, John McKeen, right, provided the funds for his research. Pfizer was the first pharmaceutical company to market the Type I Sabin Oral vaccine.

Below: In the early 1960s, Pfizer acquired almost 30 companies in many industries and a broad selection of common household consumer brands, including Barbasol shaving products.

Above: Pfizer scientist Gerald Laubach, pictured in June 1949, attracted the attention of John Powers, Jr., who put him in charge of research in the 1960s. Laubach became president in 1972.

Right: John Niblack was hired in 1967 as one of the first molecular biologists at Pfizer. He later became the company's top science officer.

others — to work on new therapies. He also introduced a "pipeline" concept in which teams would champion potential drugs through the many phases of research as they moved toward the open market. Any flaw would send the potential drug back to Discovery, which was responsible for finding compounds with potentially significant medicinal properties.

This new structure and system would enable Pfizer to generate and control an ever-expanding pipeline of new drugs. Under Laubach's leadership, the Research Division began scoring victories again. Among its first triumphs was the widely popular Vibramycin. Introduced in 1967, this medicine immediately earned accolades as a convenient once-a-day broad-spectrum antibiotic.

Your Business Is Knowledge

By 1965, Powers was looking forward to early retirement, but John McKeen's reaction was "Not so fast." Having just achieved his "5-by-5" goal, McKeen had other plans for his friend — much bigger plans. He wanted Powers to assume leadership of Pfizer. Powers agreed, and in 1965 he was appointed president and CEO, while McKeen

no concern for the core business, pharmaceuticals. All too frequently, researchers forgot that research was not an end in itself but a means to produce medicines that would generate profits for shareholders and funds for further research.

While conducting interviews and gathering information, Powers came upon Gerald Laubach, a research specialist with a revolutionary view of his field. This brilliant young organic chemist not only provided lucid answers to Powers's questions but also suggested a novel approach. In Powers's words, "He had an idea for doing research on a team basis. This seemed to me a very sound idea." In 1964, Powers appointed Laubach vice president for Medicinal Products Research.

The new vice president turned Pfizer's world upside down. Laubach completely restructured research around multidisciplinary teams, combining visions and voices from across scientific disciplines — chemists, biologists, toxicologists, and

Above: In 1968, a Pfizer sales representative in Nigeria informs a local doctor about the company's latest products.

Left: In 1965, John J. Powers, Jr., assumed the presidency of Pfizer. He had spent almost two decades traveling the world to set up Pfizer operations. As president, one of his first objectives was to bring the international operations more into sync with headquarters in New York.

Below: Pfizer's pharmaceutical lineup in the 1960s boasted some of the world's most popular medicines, including Terramycin and Tetracyn.

remained the chairman of the board and of the executive committee.

As John McKeen passed the baton to Jack Powers, the relationship between research and manufacturing came under intense scrutiny. Powers inherited a worldwide workforce of nearly 30,000 employees, including researchers, a sales force, a legal staff, and public affairs experts, as well as people who specialized in manufacturing and administrative functions. How could he knit these departments together more cohesively while simultaneously spurring Pfizer's growth?

Powers sought the guidance of Peter Drucker, the respected economist and business expert, who would become an informal advisor, sounding board, and critic. Drucker recommended that Powers hire Jean-Paul Vallès, an analyst at W.R. Grace & Company, as his assistant, to help coordinate long-range planning. Vallès would later become vice chairman of Pfizer.

The thrust of Drucker's critique, however, dealt with the way that Pfizer presented itself to the world. In studying the company's accounting methods, Drucker concluded that Pfizer was projecting a self-image based on the way it kept its books. In evaluating its costs, Pfizer acted like a

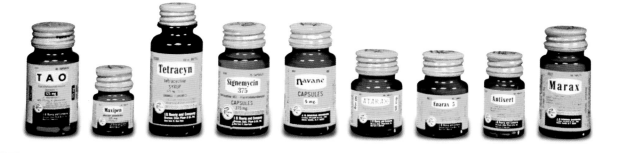

In this 1969 photo, Ed Pratt, left, tours a Pfizer facility with Bob Royer, executive vice president, Pfizer International. During Pratt's tenure as chairman and CEO, Pfizer's revenue increased sevenfold.

classic manufacturer — including amounts paid for hard material as a significant part of its final product cost. But Drucker told the company, "What you are making and selling is knowledge, and manufacturing is incidental."

Drucker observed that the physical manufacture of Pfizer's intellectual properties was a minor cost compared with the far greater expense of researching and developing them. He also believed that the gap between inappropriate accounting methods and the reality of a research-based pharmaceutical business obscured Pfizer's true nature.

As an illustration, Drucker observed that the high cost of surgery was never blamed on the price of the surgeon's scalpel. Yet, by employing accounting methods that portrayed the company as a manufacturer more than a health care provider, Pfizer had invited the very accusations of price gouging and collusion that Kefauver and the Justice Department had leveled against it.

As Pfizer moved quickly to implement Drucker's recommendations, Powers switched gears to face another fundamental challenge. During its whirlwind expansion overseas, the company had sacrificed efficiency for the sake of speed and flexibility. Powers and Dick Fenton, his successor as president of International, recognized that it was time to bring International under the wing of headquarters in New York without stemming its phenomenal growth.

They enlisted the help of Edmund T. Pratt, Jr., who had been recruited in 1964 by General J. Lawton Collins, former Army Chief of Staff and now vice chairman of the board of Pfizer International. Pratt had joined Pfizer as controller, succeeding Edwin Smith, after serving at the Pentagon, where he was Assistant Secretary of the Army for Financial Management. In 1967, Powers asked Pratt to join International to coordinate its activities with those of the domestic company, a task Pratt did not find particularly appealing:

Behind that wall there were rumors that things weren't all that great in International, particularly here in New York. Some people were leaving, and others were out looking for jobs. It was not a happy house.

Within two years, Pratt was named chairman of the board and president of Pfizer International. International was 14,000 strong and the uncontested American pharmaceutical leader in revenues overseas. But it was also running without a compass, riddled with redundancies and riven by many factions.

Under Dick Fenton, International had become a very independent, free-wheeling operation. Its board of directors functioned autonomously. Ed Pratt did not impose discipline from the parent company, but he did serve as a catalyst in integrating the two groups' managerial philosophies while retaining International's separate operations and structure. Both sides tried to become better integrated, but there were plenty of protests from division managers overseas who had been accustomed to running their own fiefdoms. Pratt saw clearly what he was up against but did not flinch:

It's not a rare situation. Most companies are affected by it. You've got to be decentralized — it's one of the facts of geography and so on. In some companies they refer to it as a "dukedom complex." Once you get a guy set down in a place abroad, pretty soon he thinks he owns it. Now he's a duke and rules the area, and you send him new products and he'll condescend to send you a report at the end of the year and tell you what your problems are. Outside of that, leave him alone.

Pratt and Powers addressed the "duke syndrome" by having the "top financial man of every location abroad report directly to New York headquarters" and by encouraging better communications among middle managers. Their efforts quickly bore fruit when direct communication between parallel divisions expedited overseas product launches.

By pulling the distant and disparate outposts of the company together, Powers prepared Pfizer for the challenges of intense global pharmaceutical competition. By appointing the brilliant Laubach as head of Research and developing a flexible "team" research model, Powers also prepared the company for a great chapter in its history: Pfizer's quantum leap in research.

In 1962, Bob Neimeth began a 34-year career with Pfizer that would take him around the world and to the top of the company's international pharmaceuticals operations. Appointed head of the International Pharmaceuticals Group in 1990, Neimeth launched innovative initiatives that helped drive the company's success in overseas markets.

This dramatic metal mosaic depicting the progress of medical science through the ages was created in 1961 by renowned metal muralist Nikos Bel-Jon for the main lobby of Pfizer's world headquarters in the heart of Manhattan.

1972: Pfizer crosses the billion-dollar sales threshold. John Powers, Jr., center, steps down as chairman; Edmund T. Pratt, Jr., right, becomes chairman and CEO; and Gerald D. Laubach becomes president.

1988: The Agricultural Division is renamed the Animal Health Division. During the next few years, the division introduces three breakthrough products: Advocin, Aviax, and Dectomax.

1990: William C. Steere, Jr., is appointed president. A year later, he becomes chief executive officer.

1982: Feldene becomes one of the largest-selling prescription anti-inflammatory medications in the world and, ultimately, Pfizer's first product to reach a total of a billion U.S. dollars in sales.

1989: Pfizer launches Procardia XL, an innovative once-a-day medication for angina and hypertension.

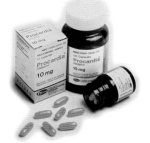

1992: Steere becomes chairman of the board. His goal is to refocus the company on its core competencies. Pfizer has triple rollout of major new drugs: Zoloft, Norvasc, and Zithromax.

SECTION III

By 1970, Pfizer had survived two tumultuous decades of controversy and rapid global expansion. It was one of the world's leaders in antibiotic research and a growing pharmaceutical company.

But the rules were changing once again. Microbiology, which sought medicines like penicillin, was gradually being replaced by organic chemistry, which relied on synthetic molecules to treat specific disease targets. Pfizer's International Division, which had been put in place so quickly, was decentralized and highly independent. And due to the frenetic pace of acquisitions, Pfizer found itself in businesses ranging from mining to metals and from toothpaste to perfume.

In the decades that followed, Pfizer intensified its investment in R&D to re-energize its pipeline and began to shed its non–health care businesses, focusing on the company's core strengths in research, development, sales, and marketing. Today, as it celebrates its 150th birthday, Pfizer is recognized as one of the leading innovators in the global pharmaceutical industry.

1993: Pfizer's Sharing the Care, the industry's premier drug-donation program, is launched. Sharing the Care has provided medicines to more than one million low-income and uninsured patients throughout the United States.

SHARING THE CARxE
A PHARMACEUTICALS ACCESS PROGRAM

1995: The Animal Health Group purchases SmithKline Beecham's animal health business, making Pfizer a world leader in the development and production of pharmaceuticals for livestock and companion animals.

1998: Pfizer's roster of outstanding drugs grows with the launch of Viagra, a breakthrough treatment for erectile dysfunction. Pfizer invests close to $2.5 billion in research.

1994: Pfizer's investment in research and development tops $1 billion annually.

1997: Pfizer is ranked the world's most admired pharmaceutical company by *Fortune* magazine. Pfizer continues its reign as most admired in 1998.

1999: At 150, Pfizer is one of the world's premier pharmaceutical companies, recognized for its success in discovering and developing innovative drugs for humans and animals. *Forbes* magazine names Pfizer "Company of the Year."

In this 1975 photograph taken at Pfizer's Central Research headquarters in Groton, Connecticut, research scientists Tom Althuis, rear, and Jasjit Bindra combine reagents in the quest for organic compounds with the potential to become new medicines.

CHAPTER ELEVEN

THE AGE OF RESEARCH

1970–1979

*We were new in the pharmaceutical industry. We had been lucky,
and with some sharp people, we had a couple of good products.... But
we weren't even spending a fraction of what Merck and other people
were.... Hell, if we were going to survive in this business, we were going
to have to be a player in their category.*

— Edmund T. Pratt, Jr., 1997

THE 1970s BEGAN WITH setbacks for Pfizer. On March 7, 1970, Pfizer lost 84-year-old George Anderson, one of its driving visionaries. Anderson's life paralleled that of his company. He had spent his boyhood watching his father serve the company's founders, Charles Pfizer and Charles Erhart. The younger Anderson had stood alongside Jasper Kane in the 1920s when Pfizer scientists mastered the process of deep-tank fermentation and the production of citric acid from fermented sugar. He had played an important role in the development of Pfizer's powerhouse products, penicillin and Terramycin. His leadership had also set the stage for Pfizer's transformation from a small fine-chemicals company into a global pharmaceutical giant. In the last five years of his life, from 1965 to 1970, he had taken great satisfaction in seeing the company's revenues nearly double, increasing from $500 million to $933 million.

As Pfizer bid farewell to Anderson, the postwar era of prosperity and economic stability also came to an end. In the early 1970s, the American economy flattened under the weight of double-digit inflation and an oil squeeze instigated by the Organization of Petroleum Exporting Countries (OPEC). As the economy contracted, factories curtailed production, gas lines lengthened, and fuel prices shot up.

While the United States struggled with its worst recession since the Great Depression, Pfizer proved once again that it could avoid being caught in the undertow. The company's fortunes were far less dependent on economic fluctuations and a buoyant stock market than on its own innovative research and worldwide marketing skills. Pfizer's ability to weather the storm demonstrated how far it had progressed toward its goal of becoming a global research-driven pharmaceutical company led by top-tier scientists working in cross-functional teams.

As had happened so often before, Pfizer was being reborn. In 1970, the board of directors formally approved changing the company's name from the old-fashioned Charles Pfizer & Company Inc. to the more modern Pfizer Inc. The company also introduced a new logo — a blue oval with the word "Pfizer" in sweeping script. Adding an exclamation point to all these changes, in 1970 the board approved the fourth stock split since the company had gone public in 1942.

This Pfizer logo was recognized around the world throughout the 1970s and 1980s. Its distinctive blue oval has remained the signature feature of Pfizer's logo, which was modernized again in 1989.

Pfizer reached $1 billion in annual sales in 1972. Shown celebrating the company's achievement are, from left, Gerald Laubach, who became president in 1972; John Powers, Jr., who retired as chairman that year; and Edmund T. Pratt, Jr., the new CEO and chairman.

In 1971, when Jack Powers announced his impending retirement, senior management began the difficult task of selecting someone to succeed him. Powers, however, had recognized the importance of succession planning. As he commented, "Many companies have been caught with a retiring leader, but without an able successor. So I began to look at successors early on."

Three candidates had emerged: Gerry Laubach, who was president of Pfizer Pharmaceuticals; Tom Cooney, who supervised consumer operations; and Ed Pratt, who was CEO of Pfizer International. The more Powers deliberated, the more he thought that the company would profit from the experience and personalities of both Laubach and Pratt:

I could visualize the possibility that while there should be one chief man, no question about that, there could be two top men in a gradually expanding organization. It was going to be pretty big and rather complicated.... In a sense, Ed Pratt and Gerry Laubach divided up the business, although

it was clear Ed was the chief executive officer. He was the boss.

In 1972, Powers stepped down, and Pratt took the reins as chairman and CEO. Laubach became president. The arrangement worked in Pfizer's favor. Pratt readily deferred to Laubach's expertise on industry problems and the more technical aspects of Pfizer's research and pharmaceutical business.

On June 29, 1973, shortly after Pratt and Laubach settled into their roles, John McKeen retired from the board of directors. McKeen's powerful presence and leadership had contributed greatly to Pfizer's growth and prosperity for nearly half a century. He left a monumental legacy. He had presided over the trailblazing research that had led to the company's breakthroughs in fermentation and its development of antibiotics. During the 1960s, he had made the strategic decision to augment internally generated growth by acquiring companies in industries ranging from medical technologies to cosmetics. And it was he who not only directed the company's emergence as a multinational corporation but also defended Pfizer with passion, eloquence, and unflinching determination during the Kefauver hearings.

When Pratt and Laubach took over, they inherited a company already generating nearly a billion dollars a year in sales, with rapidly maturing research and rising productivity. Although Pfizer was succeeding on many fronts, the new team began by addressing a larger question: What kind of company should Pfizer be? And what course could best lead to future success? They concluded that the company's competitive advantage lay in discovering, developing, and marketing innovative health care products.

The two leaders decided that Pfizer's scientific inquiry in every field and around the world should be pulled together under one umbrella. On September 23, 1971, this decision took shape in the form of Pfizer Central Research. The Groton labs became headquarters for the division, which brought together Pfizer's disparate research organizations and marked the company's increased focus on innovation as the key to success.

Chairman Ed Pratt underscored that commitment by directing that an even greater share of revenues be poured back into the labs — the engines driving the company's success. In prior years, Pfizer had typically allocated five percent or less of its budget to research and development, but Pratt was convinced that Pfizer had to plow 15 to 20 percent of its budget into R&D. He believed that such a commitment was vital if the company's productivity was to match that of the pharmaceutical industry's leading players.

Pratt's decision was controversial. Betting the bank on research meant that growth would depend on the vagaries of scientific investigation — with no guarantee of any returns. Also, a generation earlier, Pfizer scientists had needed barely a year to bring Terramycin out of the lab, but by the 1970s, government regulations and requirements for

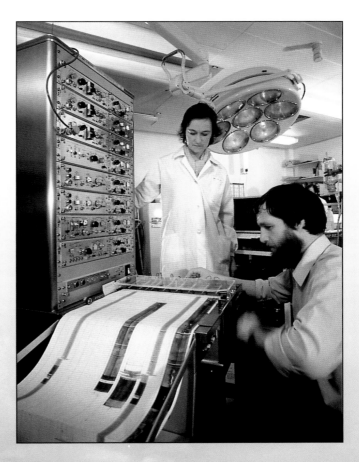

Right: In the mid-1970s, Pfizer's researchers at Sandwich, England, began searching for a new class of cardiac stimulants. These scientists were the nucleus of a cardiovascular research team that went on to discover Norvasc, which would become the world's leading cardiovascular medicine.

Below: A major laboratory expansion at Sandwich, seen here in 1975, was a manifestation of the confidence Pfizer management had in Central Research.

Above: Barry MacTaggart, president of Pfizer's International Division, right, and CEO Ed Pratt, center, are escorted around the Pfizer facility in Nagoya, Japan, during a 1971 visit.

Below: Barry Bloom became the first president of Pfizer Central Research and began to revitalize and centralize the research operation at Groton.

expanded clinical testing had lengthened the average time in development to more than a decade. Pratt recognized that Pfizer's commitment to pharmaceutical research would have to involve a long-term strategy. Nonetheless, he remained convinced that this strategy would pay off handsomely in the decades to come.

As soon as the decision to emphasize R&D was made, Central Research became an umbrella for pharmaceutical R&D, chemical research, and animal health. Barry Bloom, whom Pratt named as the first president of Pfizer Central Research, faced a daunting task. Pfizer had research labs all over the globe, a sort of United Nations with test tubes. The problem of cohesion had to be addressed once and for all. Each site presented its own

challenges, and to complicate matters further, a rivalry had developed between the labs in Groton and those in Sandwich.

Bloom realized that before the two centers could work together, morale at Sandwich would have to improve. He asked Lloyd Conover — a key figure in the discovery of tetracycline, a recipient of numerous awards, and an excellent hands-on manager — to take command at the English research site. As Conover comments:

I don't remember the words used by Barry to describe my mission, but I'm sure they went something like this: Sandwich has not been productive, report writing is terrible, morale is poor; the budgets are chronically overspent; they have too many discovery projects for the number of scientists; there are too many speculative discovery approaches. Whip Sandwich into shape.

Conover swiftly instilled discipline, coordinated assignments, and promoted talented people, triggering a transformation that would see improvements in both morale and results.

In 1979, Sandwich earned Pfizer's first Queen's Award for

Technological Achievement. It was granted for Mansil. This medicine, which had taken 10 years to develop, treated schistosomiasis, a disease caused by parasitic worms, and was 90 percent effective with just a single dose.

Next, Pfizer focused on its operations in Japan, the world's second-largest pharmaceutical market. By Japanese law, any outside company seeking to operate in the country had to have an equal Japanese partner. Pfizer had partnered with Taito Sugar Company in 1955 to manufacture and distribute antibiotics. By the 1970s, Pfizer Taito, a Pfizer subsidiary employing 1,000 people, produced bulk antibiotics and led the International

Right: Henry McKinnell joined Pfizer in Tokyo in 1971, beginning a career that would take him to the very top of the company. Over the years, Dr. McKinnell would hold positions of increasing responsibility for Pfizer operations around the world, including serving as president of Pfizer Asia, chief financial officer of Pfizer Inc, and president of the Medical Technology Group. In 1999, he was named president and chief operating officer of Pfizer.

Iwao Shino was president of Pfizer Taito for two decades.

Division in sales. Pfizer also developed a soil-screening program in labs outside Nagoya. Researchers there sent promising samples to either Groton or Sandwich for additional study.

Pfizer benefited from the favorable conditions in Japan, which included an advanced infrastructure, a solid base of technology, a stable economy, and a sophisticated system of patent protection. The latter issue was becoming increasingly important with the frequent outbreaks of drug piracy in many developing countries. Iwao Shino, who was named president and CEO of Pfizer Taito in 1971, pointed out that as late as the 1970s, Japan was one of a select group of nations that recognized and protected the value of intellectual property:

Japan has product patent protection for pharmaceuticals. As long as the patent is in effect, companies don't have to worry. For instance, Vibramycin was well protected; every time competitors began to import imitations from Spain and other countries in Europe, we went after them, and none of those products was allowed in the country.

Pfizer also established 44 scholarships that were awarded to students at each medical school in Japan. According to Shino, "In this way, the Pfizer name was rapidly established within the government, medical associations, and medical schools." After 1961, when Japan guaranteed universal health coverage and a national pension for every citizen, Pfizer became adept in dealing

In addition to the labs in Groton, Connecticut; Sandwich, England; and Nagoya, Japan, this lab in Amboise, France, was brought into Central Research. The facility was originally devoted to toxicology tests of new compounds.

Below: Craig Saxton, M.D., who joined Pfizer's operations in Sandwich, England, in 1976 and became executive vice president of Central Research in 1993, is convinced that one of Pfizer's core strengths is the global presence and cultural diversity gained through the company's worldwide network of clinical centers.

with the country's complicated health care delivery system.

At the same time, Pfizer's international headquarters operations supported the overseas divisions through four worldwide management centers. Victor Micati, a product manager with Pfizer International who would later become executive vice president of the Pfizer Pharmaceuticals Group, said the management centers provided more than just support for far-flung operations:

These management centers served as wonderful training grounds for our people. They were intermediary positions. You could move people out of markets into a regional operation in some kind of functional capacity or cross-functional capacity, and it really represented an important source of talent.

The final component of the new Central Research organization was a laboratory in Amboise, France. Founded in 1970, the Amboise site was dedicated almost entirely to evaluating drugs discovered in Sandwich and, to a lesser extent, in Groton.

In addition to fundamentally restructuring its research organization, Pfizer also fine-tuned its basic thrust. The company decided to radically de-emphasize fermentation research in favor of synthetic organic chemistry as a potential source of new medicines. Extensive use of interdisciplinary teams, initiated by Laubach, continued to speed processes and encourage the cross-fertilization of ideas.

All told, Pfizer invested more than a billion dollars in research during the 1970s. Ed Pratt believed that ideas are the most precious capital a company can have, and he was convinced that investing at unprecedented levels was necessary to create innovative, value-added therapies capable of meeting unmet medical needs. By making research Pfizer's lodestar, he enabled the company to reinvent and recast itself in the 1970s as a modern research organization.

Pratt's strategy proved correct. Two decades later, Pfizer would unveil an astonishing array of outstanding medicines. In many cases, the research projects that yielded them had begun more than 10 years earlier:

- Research into Zithromax, a powerful antibiotic introduced in 1992, began in 1974.
- The development of Feldene, an anti-inflammatory which, by itself, fueled the company's growth throughout the 1980s, started in the late 1960s, but only blossomed in the 1970s.
- Research on Norvasc, Pfizer's top-selling drug, which was approved in 1992, began more than a decade earlier.
- Zoloft, the antidepressant medicine that was approved in the United States in 1992, began in Discovery in 1978.

An Agricultural Division sales representative talks to a farmer in the Philippines about Liquamycin, which gained wide acceptance in international markets in the 1970s.

The great sweep of Pfizer's reforms left no corner of the business untouched. In 1975, Ed Pratt offered Lloyd Conover the opportunity to organize the research operation of the Agricultural Products Division. Like many other Pfizer divisions, Agricultural Products enjoyed robust growth. Operating initially on a shoestring budget, it had grown into a multimillion-dollar business, but it had no agreed-upon business plan for the future.

Conover accepted the challenge, although he explained, "I took the job with some misgivings. Animal health research had always been a poor relation in what was basically a human-drug research organization. Budgets had been held essentially at a no-growth level for several years."

Before long, he had infused new life into Agriculture. The division scored successes with drugs like Mecadox, a treatment for bacterial infections, and Banminth, for parasite control in swine. A combination of Banminth and Mecadox became the most successful feed additive for pigs in the United States.

At the same time, a joint team working in Groton, Terre Haute, and Sandwich developed an injectable form of Terramycin. Called Terramycin/LA in international markets and Liquamycin LA-200 in Canada and the United States, this new

variation on Terramycin represented a substantial improvement over earlier less-potent medications because a single injection was effective for up to three days. It went on to become one of the Agricultural Division's best-sellers.

As new drugs rolled out of Pfizer's expanding pipeline, the company realized that it had to refine its structure and strengthen its overall approach to selling pharmaceuticals. Pfizer had learned that even the most promising drugs needed comprehensive support to become blockbusters.

Educating the Public

However, the U.S. government's expanding role meant that the days of moving drugs almost directly from the lab to the market were over. In the United States, pharmaceutical companies faced countless obstacles in the form of a bureaucratic FDA, an increasingly litigious society, and a more complex health care system. The time had come for Pfizer to blaze a new trail for the industry, using a strengthened Public Affairs Division to educate the public about the obstacles that were keeping pharmaceuticals from reaching patients.

Pfizer did not have to start from scratch. In the 1960s, the company had established a Public Affairs Division, with an office in Washington, D.C. Before retiring in 1972, Jack Powers observed that "public affairs was a concern, because by that time, I'd seen plenty of government overregulation. Much of it was the result of a poor public image of this industry, a holdover from the Kefauver days. It seemed that it was very important to correct that image."

Powers summoned Public Affairs Director Edward Littlejohn to his office, and the two agreed to completely revamp the division. Littlejohn recommended that Pfizer study the complicated process of moving a drug from the lab to the consumer and evaluate each constraint individually. He also pointed out the lag in getting drugs approved in the United States. Those approvals often came long after Pfizer International had established a drug in markets overseas.

Littlejohn said, "If we could show that people were dying in the United States from heart conditions because the drugs weren't available, and if the death rate had gone down in the United Kingdom,

then [we could show that] our regulations were not saving lives, but killing people."

Pfizer wasted no time in mounting an aggressive public relations campaign. In 1974, Senator Edward Kennedy held hearings on his proposed bill to tighten regulatory policy on the pharmaceutical industry. Gerry Laubach and Paul Miller, Pfizer's future general counsel, represented the company during the hearings. In his testimony, Laubach refused to cede the higher ground to Kennedy, demonstrating that the constraints placed upon drug research by government regulation are the most significant cause of this slowdown, particularly constraints upon the early innovative phases of drug research. Laubach explained:

As the cost of developing new drugs escalates, funds available for discovering new drugs inevitably decline. The higher the cost of drug development and the more expensive and demanding the clinical test requirements, the more funds are drained away from supporting the innovation process.

The issue was not to be easily resolved. Overregulation and lag time continued to plague the pharmaceutical industry, and Pfizer was obliged to devote increasing time and resources to meeting requirements that were part of the FDA's lengthy approval process.

Beyond pharmaceuticals, Pfizer was now a vastly different company. During the diversification program of the 1960s, Pfizer had acquired a host of new businesses, ranging from chemicals for paper products to cosmetics. In the 1970s, Pfizer modified its acquisition strategy, looking for more

Above: Paul Miller, who later became Pfizer's general counsel, successfully represented Pfizer during congressional hearings in the 1970s.

medical technology businesses to complement its strength in pharmaceuticals. The company took a major step when, in 1972, it acquired Howmedica, Inc., an international manufacturer renowned for high-quality dental products, hospital products, and orthopedic devices — including a widely used hip prosthesis. The Howmedica acquisition, for which Pfizer paid more than three million shares of its own stock, was at the time the largest in the company's history. In 1979, Pfizer moved further into the hospital products market with the acquisition of Shiley, Inc. Founded in 1964 in California, Shiley had pioneered a mechanical heart valve and other cardiovascular-related products.

In 1976, as America celebrated its 200th birthday with fireworks and tall ships in New York harbor, Pfizer celebrated 125 years of explosive growth. Around the world, Pfizer's more than 40,000 employees worked at facilities in 40 nations.

Central Research continued to explore new products in a wide variety of therapeutic areas and to refine its approach to science. The division

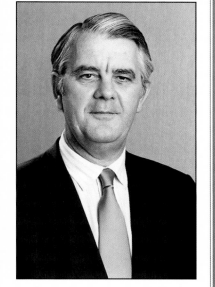

Right: Nigel Gray joined Howmedica in England in 1975, three years after it became a Pfizer subsidiary. An architect of Howmedica's success, he became president of Pfizer's Medical Technology Group in 1995 and later led its businesses through divestiture, ensuring their successful transition by maintaining both morale and value.

Below: With an eye toward the future, teams of scientists throughout Pfizer laboratories began working on projects in the 1970s that would result in blockbuster drugs introduced many years later. Pictured is a laboratory at the company's research facility in Sandwich, England.

also celebrated a more immediate victory. Pfizer had just won FDA approval for Minipress, a new medicine for high blood pressure that produced fewer side effects than other cardiovascular drugs.

Pfizer's 1976 annual report highlighted the company's research products and capabilities:

Pfizer Inc is a worldwide research-based company with primary interests in pharmaceuticals and hospital products (including orthopedic prosthetic devices, medical specialties and surgical equipment, diagnostic systems, and radiographic technology). Other major product lines include organic fine chemicals (for food, beverage, pharmaceutical, and industrial applications), agricultural products (animal health products and seed, and poultry operations), consumer products (fragrances, cosmetics, and other health and beauty products), and materials science products (industrial specialties and minerals).

In a special section entitled "Where have we been? Where are we going? A Discussion with Members of Pfizer Management," Ed Pratt summed up Pfizer in the 1970s:

I think that the decentralization of International was one of the key factors in our outstanding success abroad. At the moment, we are something of a mixed breed. We have maintained the International Division concept for certain parts of our business — pharmaceutical, agricultural, and chemical — but we've gone the one-world route with several other operations, such as Consumer and Howmedica. We've tried to be responsive to what we feel are the

Above: Bob Brown, vice president, Employee Resources, joined Pfizer in 1970. A staunch advocate of innovative employee resources practices, Brown spearheaded an effort that would earn Pfizer the U.S. Department of Labor's Exemplary Voluntary Efforts (EVE) award in 1992. Pfizer was honored by Secretary of Labor Lynn Martin for the outstanding and multifaceted programs the company has put in place to enhance employment opportunities for all employees.

Left: This photo taken in France in the early 1970s captures the carefully controlled production procedures used by Pfizer around the world to assure the sterility of an injectable product.

needs and opportunities in the individual situations without taking a doctrinaire approach.

Ed Pratt had set Pfizer on a new course. With his first decade as CEO drawing to a close, everyone in the company was cheered by Pfizer's enormous progress. The company had reorganized, expanded, and revitalized its divisions; it had refined its approach to acquisitions; and it had gained entry into the exclusive club of America's 100 largest companies.

Sadly, the decade ended — just as it had begun — with the loss of one of Pfizer's strongest leaders. John McKeen, the man responsible for transforming Pfizer into a global company, died in 1978 at 75 years of age. The company's annual report described the magnitude of his contribution:

As this annual report went to press, we were deeply saddened by the death on February 24, 1978, of John McKeen, whose drive and vision transformed Pfizer from a small fine-chemicals house into a major company with operations throughout the world. Under his leadership, sales grew from $47.5 million in 1949 to more than $542 million in 1965.... In Pfizer's 129-year history, no one has had a greater impact on the growth and progress of the company than John McKeen.

By 1979, Pfizer was a $2.7 billion company with a research budget of nearly $140 million. The largest United States–based pharmaceutical firm abroad, Pfizer became increasingly concerned about global threats to its intellectual property.

In 1995, the Harvard Business School released a study entitled "Pfizer: Global Protection of Intellectual Property" that described the company's worldwide effort to protect brain-based industries:

With the chairmanship of Ed Pratt beginning in 1972, Pfizer increased its emphasis on developing new and innovative proprietary drugs. During this period, marked by steady increases in research spending, Pfizer became a pharmaceutical innovator.... In the 1970s, after solving its patent enforcement problems in Europe, Pfizer's efforts turned to Less Developed Countries (LDCs). These markets had by then become important for Pfizer, and lack of patent protection had emerged as a problem in countries such as Mexico, Brazil, Argentina, and

Over the decades, Pfizer has become renowned for its marketing prowess. Here, Bill Steere, left, then president of U.S. Pharmaceuticals, works on an ad campaign in the late 1980s with Gary Jortner, now head of product development for Pfizer Pharmaceuticals.

India. Gone were the days when lack of infrastructure and technical know-how had protected Pfizer's patents in LDCs.

Pfizer's focus on protecting intellectual property globally served as a touchstone that indicated both where the company had been and where it was going. This focus grew in part out of Pfizer's greater commitment to R&D and its increasing success in bringing to market outstanding innovative drugs. The company's advocacy of intellectual property protection also reflected its increasing effort to address issues of policy and governmental regulation both in the United States and abroad. Pfizer's decisive leadership in the intellectual property arena marked its full-fledged entry into the international field as a player of global importance. In the coming decades, Pfizer would increase its commitment to R&D, become a leader in innovation, speak for the industry in many policy and regulatory debates, and emerge as one of the world's preeminent health care companies.

A Pfizer scientist studies a chromatograph of DNA under ultraviolet light.

CHAPTER TWELVE

THE PIPELINE

1980–1989

I remember we talked about growing Central Research at 20 percent a year to make sure that we had all the resources necessary as we moved through the eighties into the nineties. Looking back, that decision was very critical because those new products were significantly funded throughout the eighties and resulted in new products that we have been rolling out around the world today.

— Brian Barrett, 1997

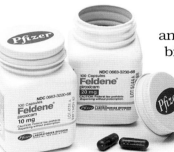

AS THE 1980s BEGAN, MILLIONS of people around the world with arthritis, diabetes, cardiovascular disorders, mental illness, and other diseases were benefiting from Pfizer products. The company's sales were thriving. Pfizer's billion-dollar gamble — investing substantially in scientific research — was beginning to pay off for the company and for patients around the globe. While the words "the world's leading pharmaceutical company" had not yet been uttered publicly, Pfizer was driving toward that goal, and CEO Ed Pratt continued to invest ever greater resources in Central Research.

Throughout the 1980s, Pfizer achieved its dual goal of improving health care while providing excellent returns to its shareholders. Sales for 1980 exceeded $3 billion, with net income surpassing $250 million. Pfizer International continued to be the strongest engine for growth, with combined sales of Minipress and the anti-arthritic drug Feldene exceeding those of all drugs sold by Pfizer in the United States, the world's largest pharmaceutical market.

Buoyed by this success, Pratt asked Pfizer's board to approve a bold, long-term strategy driven by innovative research. Dubbed "Pfizer in the 1980s," the program called for 20 percent annual increases in Central Research's budget. Pratt also announced Pfizer's plan to spend $1 billion on capital expansion between 1981 and 1985, including a $50 million upgrade that would enable the Groton research facility to accommodate several hundred new employees.

The 1980s began with 15 new Pfizer products working their way through the approval process at the FDA. Lag time at that agency had resulted in drugs like Minipress and Feldene being launched first overseas, then coming to the United States with established sales histories. Bill Steere, then general manager of Pfizer Laboratories, remarked that Pfizer was at the start of a "new cycle." As he recognized:

We were being hit with the continued erosion of Sinequan, Navane, Diabinese, Vibramycin, Antivert, Antarax — all the products of the 1960s and 1970s — which were going off patent. They were Pfizer 10 years ago. Then, a whole new portfolio of products was going to be Pfizer today.

First approved in some overseas markets in 1980 and in the United States two years later, Feldene became Pfizer's most successful internally developed drug to date and provided much-needed revenue.

The Logjam

By 1980, Bill Steere had been with the company 21 years. His performance had attracted the notice of senior management, which had entrusted him with increasingly important assignments. When only a 27-year-old product manager, he had been charged with supervising the company's marketing in Latin America. Having successfully completed this assignment, he was promoted to vice president of marketing for Pfizer's Roerig Division, then made general manager of Roerig and a few years later of Pfizer Laboratories.

Bill Steere understood that the company's prosperity depended upon speeding up the process that moved drugs from the laboratory to the marketplace. In the early 1980s, Procardia (a breakthrough treatment for angina), Cefobid (a broadspectrum antibiotic marketed overseas as Bacacil), Mansil (developed at Sandwich to combat the parasitic disease schistosomiasis), and Feldene (to treat arthritis) were all awaiting FDA approval.

Expectations for these drugs were high. Pfizer felt confident that, by 1985, sales would increase

by as much as $1 billion. In 1980, Mansil became the first drug to clear regulatory review — followed by Procardia. Pfizer had licensed Procardia from the German firm Bayer as the first oral formulation of a new family of heart medications called calcium channel blockers. These medicines prevent coronary spasms by blocking the flow of calcium ions that might otherwise promote contractions of the coronary artery muscles. FDA Commissioner Arthur Hayes, Jr., hailed Procardia as "a significant medical advance for patients who can't tolerate or aren't helped by other drugs," such as beta blockers and nitroglycerin.

The Wall Street Journal reported that many physicians working with calcium channel blockers predicted that they would be effective in treating angina. That prediction came true, and demand exploded. In March 1982 alone, physicians wrote

Above: Feldene, the first once-a-day drug for osteoarthritis and rheumatoid arthritis, was introduced in the United States in 1982 by the Pfizer Labs field force. On hand to celebrate the drug's launch were William "B.J." Robison, who was then vice president of Sales; Bill Steere, who was senior vice president and general manager; and Karen Katen, who was director of Product Management.

Left: Some of Feldene's principal scientists are shown with the volumes of data required for its New Drug Application filed with the FDA. From left: Robert Proctor, Edward Wiseman, and Joseph Lombardino.

152,000 prescriptions for Procardia. In its first 12 weeks on the market, Procardia sales totaled $17 million and, in its first year, more than $81 million.

Three months later, Pfizer followed this breakthrough with Feldene, a blockbuster synthetic drug that provided relief for arthritis sufferers. Generically known as piroxicam, this once-a-day anti-arthritis medication was a major achievement for Pfizer scientists. Feldene was the company's first synthetic drug to generate huge sales. It was also the only once-a-day dosage treatment for arthritis available anywhere. Doctors extolled Feldene's low dose, once-daily dosage, and high efficacy.

Right: A 37-year Pfizer veteran, Controller Herbert Ryan has led the company to prominence in the area of financial reporting and disclosure. As a result, Pfizer is now recognized as a leader in financial reporting among its peers, in the financial community, and in the governmental regulatory arena.

Below: In 1989, Pfizer launched a media campaign to raise public awareness about arthritis. Using the Tin Man from the classic movie *The Wizard of Oz* as its centerpiece, the program urged people with arthritis symptoms to see their doctor. Flanking the metallic luminary are members of the marketing team that created the campaign, Randi Goldmann, James Bargon, and Laurie Olson.

True to tradition, Pfizer launched an impressive marketing campaign to educate the public, physicians, and other health care professionals about Feldene. Feldene's worldwide sales broke all Pfizer records, easily making it the company's number one product.

Building a Better Pipeline

The success of Procardia and Feldene gave Central Research the freedom to grow but also demonstrated the need for better organization. Building a world-class drug pipeline from the ground up required careful stewardship of millions of dollars, sophisticated equipment, mastery of diverse scientific disciplines, and better integration with the sales and marketing arms. John Niblack, then vice president of Medicinal Products Research, described the situation:

In the mid-eighties, it became obvious that in a company as big as Pfizer, we had too big a gap between the R&D operations and the needs of the sales and marketing groups. Marketing had certain ideas about what it wanted, how it wanted a product developed, and what attributes and features it wanted highlighted in a development program. That requires a lot of preplanning because once these development programs are launched, you can't change them very easily, and you don't want to go back and do additional studies because you add more time to the development process.

Pfizer devised a deceptively simple solution: It established Early Candidate Management Teams, with representatives from research, marketing, and sales. Later-stage development projects could then be handed off to an Advanced Candidate Management Team chaired by a marketing person. Together, these teams would plan Pfizer's development programs and report to centralized management committees.

Groton became the official headquarters of Pfizer Research. Each discovery project had an operating plan with clearly defined goals, timelines, and milestones. Central Research and the U.S. Pharmaceuticals Group were the first to experiment with the new system. Bill Steere, named president of USPG in 1986, remembers that the goal was to plan for the future:

We started to break down the silos between these businesses. Working with John Niblack and Barry Bloom, we established a matrix between U.S. Pharmaceuticals and Central Research. It was the first time this had been done. Our goal was to communicate earlier on products to make sure that their development was such that when they entered the market, they'd be instant successes.

As Central Research and marketing moved closer together, the company decided to look more critically at the structure of Pfizer International. Advancing technology, falling trade barriers, and the new global economy were influencing Pfizer to reassess its global operations. Already, research management in Groton worked closely with the labs in England, France, and Japan, and the Early Candidate Management Teams evaluated a medication's potential worldwide.

Pfizer's global market increasingly resembled an interwoven tapestry that could be most profitably served through better coordination and planning. By 1984, Barry MacTaggart, president and chairman of the International Division, had concluded that Pfizer's long tradition of decentralization was no longer in the company's best interests, and he closed down Pfizer's four international management centers.

In the early 1980s, Pfizer Chairman and CEO Edmund Pratt announced a $50 million expansion of the Groton research labs. At the dedication ceremonies in 1985, Pfizer employees gathered outside to celebrate.

Above: Pfizer managers work across divisions, gathering and focusing the company's expertise on the challenges of a changing global marketplace. Here, members of Pfizer's cross-divisional Pharmaceuticals Steering Committee discuss strategies. From left: Peter Brandt, Chuck Dombeck, Fred Telling, Karen Katen, and team chair George Milne.

Right: Edmund Pratt, center, celebrates the Cefobid licensing agreement with Japanese officials. Clockwise from Pratt, are Toyama President Nakano, Robert Feeney, Fred Uememura, Barry MacTaggart, David Johnston, Tom Connors, and Lou Clemente. As vice president of Licensing and Development, Robert Feeney led the effort to license Cefobid as well as other important products, including the cardiovascular medicine Procardia.

Knowledge Is Power

As Pfizer streamlined its global efforts, Pratt led an international drive for intellectual property protection. He felt compelled to spearhead this initiative because so many developing markets recognized no such rights. Since products could be increasingly copied in a simple chemistry lab with the right "recipe," other firms often pirated Pfizer medicines even before the company could bring them to market. In 1981, for example, when Pfizer introduced Feldene in Argentina, two local companies were already selling it. Pfizer had devoted 20 years of research and had invested many millions of dollars to develop and distribute

Feldene, but the Argentinean government neither recognized the company's patent nor made any effort to prevent local businesses from manufacturing and selling the drug.

In a 1985 speech to the Newcomen society, Pratt spoke of the rampant intellectual property theft that Pfizer faced:

> *In Greece, we filed suit in 1981 against a pirate manufacturer of Feldene who was using a process we had patented under local law. Four years elapsed before we received a favorable ruling. Although we won the battle, we certainly lost the war. Patent protection of our process has now expired, and the copier is now legally free to continue copying our product. These types of situations are not uncommon in many developing nations.*

Pratt soon gained a reputation as one of the world's great defenders of patents and intellectual property. Knowing the battle would be won or lost in the halls of government, he used his influence in Washington to raise the profile of intellectual property as a major economic issue. In 1982, Pratt joined the U.S. private sector advisory group at the

General Agreement on Tariffs and Trade (GATT) negotiations. He enlisted the help of other companies suffering from property theft — including Merck, Johnson & Johnson, Bristol-Myers, and IBM — and together they formed the Intellectual Property Committee (IPC).

A Harvard Business School study saluted the IPC for "forging an unusual tripartite coalition among European, Japanese, and United States industry to work with their respective governments to secure global protection for intellectual property through the GATT."

Unfortunately, progress was not speedy, and rampant intellectual theft countered any growth generated by new drugs during the second half of the decade. International business was very tough. Feldene, Pfizer's major product, was under constant attack from legitimate competitors as well as international pirates, and as a result, it fell from third place in the global marketplace to nineteenth.

Pfizer faced other competitive pressures as well. Unburdened by the cost of research, development, and clinical trials, generic companies waited until a patent expired, then followed the recipe in the original patent, selling the resultant medicine at prices well below those of the company that had discovered and developed the drug. Even more frustrating, by 1978 the average time needed to discover and develop new drugs to meet the FDA's expanded requirements and then undergo regulatory review had reached 14 years or more. At the same time, costs connected with the approval process increased tenfold. Meanwhile, the length of time covered by patents — then 17 years — remained the same.

When the Drug Price Competition and Patent Restoration Act of 1984, sponsored by Congressman Henry Waxman and Senator Orrin Hatch, passed, the generic companies got even more of a boost. The new law had two provisions — one substantially helping the generic companies and the other aiding research-based pharmaceutical companies. This legislation permitted manufacturers to file Abbreviated New Drug Applications for generic versions of all pharmaceutical products approved after 1962. The generic manufacturers had only to verify that their product was therapeutically equivalent to the branded version. The law also permitted innovators like Pfizer to calculate how much time had been spent in the research, investigative, and registration phases. Once a drug gained approval, its patent was extended by half the investigative time and the full amount of

Diflucan, the first Pfizer drug to be launched in the 1990s, has since become the world's leading prescription antifungal. Here, a Roerig medical service representative receives medical and market-specific training on Diflucan prior to the drug's introduction.

time spent in registration. No drug, however, was permitted more than 14 years of patent life.

This act opened the floodgates, and more than 1,000 applications were filed in the first year alone. Within a decade, the generic industry increased its sales to nearly $1 billion as patents expired on numerous products.

Faced with a generic challenge to its core brands, Pfizer sought to innovate through diversification. By the 1980s, Pfizer's hospital and diagnostic products were second in importance only to its pharmaceuticals, and the Hospital Products Group accounted for almost $1 billion in sales. Howmedica, the group's largest division, marketed orthopedic hip replacements such as those implanted in Pope John Paul II and former football and baseball star Bo Jackson. Other market leaders included Deknatel's cardiovascular sutures and thoracic drainage devices and Shiley's heart valve implants and blood oxygenators. Howmedica opened research centers in Ireland and Groton and purchased the French company Jaquet Frères, which produced fixation devices like splints and crutches.

Throughout the decade, Pfizer expanded the Hospital Products Group with a wide range of acquisitions:
- Valleylab, Inc., a manufacturer of medical equipment such as electrosurgical systems and intravenous pumps;
- Stockert Instruments, a German manufacturer of heart-lung blood pumps used during open-heart surgery;
- Schneider Medintag, a Swiss manufacturer of angioplasty products such as balloon catheters used to dilate narrowed arteries; and
- American Medical Systems, creator of a line of urological devices to treat both impotence and incontinence.

The mid-1980s held much promise for Pfizer's subsidiary, Shiley, Inc., which introduced a new oxygenator and new heart valves that were well received by the medical community. However, by 1984, problems had developed with Shiley's 60-degree Convexo-Concave heart valve, which failed in a very small number of recipients. Pfizer removed the product from the market, and although these

Left: As head of Pfizer's worldwide manufacturing operations, John Mitchell, who joined Pfizer in 1964 at the Brooklyn plant, is responsible for the company's globally integrated production network.

In 1969, Pfizer began construction of a plant in Ringaskiddy, Ireland. It was the company's single largest investment outside of the United States. In 2001, Pfizer will open a new $300 million bulk pharmaceutical products facility at the site.

valves had saved many thousands of lives, and nearly 99 percent had functioned as expected, the company agreed to settle a worldwide class-action suit filed in the U.S. District Court in Cincinnati, Ohio, in 1992. Under the settlement, the company established a consultation fund of between $90 million and $140 million (depending on the number of claims filed) to cover the cost of patient consultations with cardiologists and other health care specialists, and a second fund of at least $75 million for valve-related research to identify patients who had a "significant risk of fracture and for certain types of unreimbursed medical expenses." Pfizer's General Counsel Paul Miller observed, "Never before has a company taken such a step to set aside a complex and time-consuming litigation and redirect its energies and resources to the benefit of its product users."

By 1993, Pfizer was dealing with the approximately 900 implantees who had opted out of the settlement. Within a year, the vast majority of cases had been resolved, and Shiley was ultimately sold to the Fiat subsidiary Sorin Biomedica S.p.A. for $230 million.

Pfizer's Divisions

Pfizer did not allow the Shiley litigation to derail its plans for growth in its other operations. The Consumer Products Division achieved new heights, helping consumers enjoy everything from clearer eyes (Visine eye drops) to a better night's sleep (Unisom sleep aids) to improved oral hygiene (Plax) to added beauty (Coty's Sophia line of perfumes and toiletries, named for movie star Sophia Loren).

Meanwhile, the Agricultural Division was focused on investing in research. A new animal health research center at Terre Haute was completed in 1982, and animal health research operations in Sandwich were joined with those in the United States to form one organization. In addition to a strong discovery effort, the organization was focused on the development of three important new drugs:

- Advocin, a broad-spectrum antibiotic that treats respiratory diseases in cattle, swine, and poultry;
- Aviax, to treat coccidiosis, a disease common in broiler chickens and caged laying hens; and
- Dectomax, for the control of parasites in livestock.

In anticipation of promising new medicines like Cardura and Diflucan, Roerig executives gathered in 1989 to plan an expansion that would double Roerig's field force in a year. From left: Peter Brandt, Hank McCrorie, Bill Canata, and Karen Katen, then vice president and director of operations for Roerig.

Although animal health medicines were subject to many of the same FDA constraints as human pharmaceuticals, the situation in this field was even worse. Whereas a drug such as Terramycin needed only one clearance for a particular human application, animal medicines required multiple approvals for different species. When Terramycin was approved for swine, it still had to be separately tested and approved for poultry, cattle, and other livestock. Despite the fact that Pfizer's worldwide animal health sales were small compared to human pharmaceuticals sales, they exceeded $500 million by 1988, making Pfizer the leader in the field.

The 1980s were also a period of transition for the Chemical Division. In late 1981, Pfizer veterans Frank Adams and Donald Kolowsky were given responsibility for integrating the company's many chemical entities worldwide. Under their guidance, the Chemical Division also made headway, developing new products like Alitame, which was many times sweeter than other sweetening agents available at the time.

Alitame had the potential to be a stellar addition to Pfizer's product line. Following the company's formal submission of its application to the FDA in the summer of 1986, however, rats used in the testing developed abnormal liver conditions and Alitame's prospects fell into limbo. The impasse lasted throughout the decade, with the FDA unwilling to approve the substance or to declare it a danger. But the disappointment with Alitame was offset by an unexpected opportunity to produce beta-thymidine, an intermediate for making AZT, the premier product in the treatment of AIDS.

The Next Generation of Medicines

Thanks to its new medicines, especially Feldene and Procardia, and its ongoing commitment to research, Pfizer enjoyed growing sales throughout the 1980s. By the end of the decade, organic chemists, who synthesized molecules, dominated Pfizer's drug discovery, and scientists were uncovering the molecular basis of many diseases.

As the decade ended, Pfizer's pipeline was bursting with new drugs. In 1989, the FDA approved Procardia XL, the first once-a-day calcium channel blocker for angina and hypertension. This product, Pfizer's first major launch in eight years, had outstanding market potential.

The drug was a product of high-science technology. A new osmotic push-pull pump in a pill developed by ALZA and licensed by Pfizer allowed the medicine to be released at a near-constant rate, giving patients round-the-clock protection with a single dose.

At the 1987 launch meeting for a new Pfizer antibiotic, Unasyn, members of the company's Roerig field force learn how the drug will be positioned in the hospital marketplace.

Pfizer scientist Anne Schmidt uses a cell harvester to conduct a receptor-binding assay. The test is used for finding antidepressant therapies. Zoloft, an antidepressant, was one of three innovative drugs, along with Norvasc and Zithromax, that Pfizer introduced in 1992.

CHAPTER THIRTEEN

THE TRIUMVIRATE

So one molecular change went from a laboratory curiosity to a drug that sold $600 million worldwide in 1995.

— Mike Bright, 1995

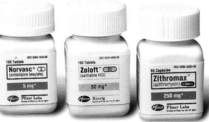

PFIZER'S PHENOMENAL success in the early 1990s was a direct result of linking Central Research with marketing and sales, combining the company's strength in discovering and developing pharmaceuticals with its expertise in marketing them. In 1992, Pfizer's research and marketing prowess helped lift three drugs to blockbuster status: Zoloft, Zithromax, and Norvasc. Amazingly, Pfizer achieved this feat within the space of 10 months.

When Norvasc was launched in the United States in 1992 as a treatment for angina and hypertension, it was already the leading calcium channel blocker in half the countries in which it had been introduced. Norvasc was a blessing for patients with chronic heart problems because, unlike other calcium channel blockers, it could be used to treat angina and hypertensive patients who also had mild-to-moderate congestive heart failure.

Before Pfizer could market Norvasc, it needed to expand its marketing and sales team. To accommodate Pfizer's burgeoning number of products, Pratt Pharmaceuticals was created. William "B.J." Robison, then vice president of sales for Pfizer Laboratories, took on the challenge of creating this new sales division.

Norvasc proved to be one of Pfizer's most successful drugs. By 1997, it had become the only drug in Pfizer's history to surpass $2 billion in annual sales. Even after four years on the U.S. market, Norvasc sales were growing at an annual rate of 23 percent, exceeding Zoloft sales — Pfizer's next highest seller — by $700 million.

The research that led to Norvasc had begun in 1979 at Sandwich under the guidance of Roger Burges. More than 1,500 compounds were tested over two years before the Burges team finally discovered amlodipine, later trademarked as Norvasc. Norvasc was approved for overseas markets in 1990 and received domestic approval in 1992.

Like Norvasc, Zoloft, an antidepressant, was launched in the United States in 1992. This medicine helps regulate the brain's serotonin levels without causing the debilitating side effects of many antidepressants, Zoloft was enthusiastically received, reaching $1.5 billion in annual sales in its fifth year on the market. This drug has also been spotlighted by the national media and by public figures who have given first-hand testimony concerning its effectiveness in fighting depression and anxiety. Willard Welch, who

Three Pfizer blockbusters: Norvasc, the world's leading antihypertensive; Zoloft, the number two antidepressant; and Zithromax, the most prescribed oral antibiotic in the United States.

developed the molecule with fellow pharmacologist Ken Koe, remembers an especially moving testimonial at a dinner given to celebrate Zoloft's launch in the United States:

I was invited to a banquet hosted by NARSAD [National Association for Research in Schizophrenia and Depression] in early October 1996. My wife looked over to the next table and Mike Wallace was there. He had been on "Larry King Live" with Art Buchwald, and they have all suffered from depression. Mike Wallace, on the program, said Zoloft had saved his life. So Ken and I got up from the table after the awards and went over to meet him. We told him who we were, and we got some pictures that we will treasure ... for a long time.

After Zoloft came Zithromax, the second pharmaceutical in the 1992 triple rollout. Unlike many antibiotics, Zithromax treats most respiratory infections in adults and children with once-daily dosing for just five days. In 1998, sales of Zithromax increased to more than $1 billion, making this azilide antibiotic Pfizer's first billion-dollar anti-infective.

Zithromax grew out of the effort Pfizer began in the mid-1970s to improve the erythromycin molecule. During the project's first 10 years, a team of 30 Pfizer scientists repeatedly modified the molecule, but with no success. Finally, however, they

---

Left: William "B.J." Robison, executive vice president, Corporate Employee Resources, who has been in Pfizer sales for more than 30 years, was chosen to start up the new Pratt Pharmaceuticals division and also helped launch Norvasc, Pfizer's all-time best-selling drug.

Below: Medical service representatives play an important role in keeping physicians abreast of the latest research findings. In Orvieto, Italy, a Pfizer representative, right, informs a specialist about a recently introduced Pfizer pharmaceutical.

learned of a breakthrough technique used by a Yugoslavian company, Pliva Pharmaceuticals, which had succeeded in incorporating a basic nitrogen ring into the erythromycin molecule. The resulting compound was enormously potent. Pfizer scientists then turned their attention to finding an orally active derivative. Mike Bright, a Pfizer researcher, describes what happened next:

If we could find out what type of changes would give us oral activity, we could have our own patent because that would be an improvement over the Pliva compound. I started the molecule-by-molecule changes myself, with my wonderful lab assistant, Richard Watrous. It took us about eight months, and we sent it to Dr. Rachel Mason for testing. And, hey, lookee here.... In the test tubes, we were killing all the bugs that the original compound did, and we were killing the haemophilus robustly. Next, we put it into infected animals by oral administration.... We were sweating it out. At the end of six days, the animals were all alive and doing great. Seven days later, they were fine. Bottom line, bingo. So one molecular change went from a laboratory curiosity to a drug that sold $600 million worldwide in 1995.

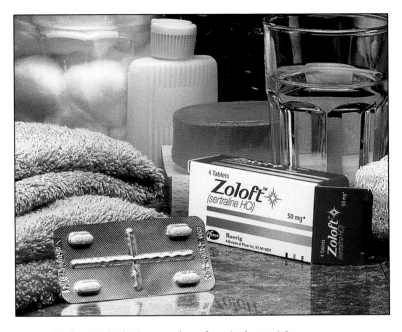

Above: Zoloft, a leader in the new class of serotonin reuptake inhibitors, was introduced in 1992, 15 years after it was synthesized.

Below left: Norvasc, Pfizer's once-daily calcium channel blocker, is the world's number one antihypertensive and the largest-selling drug in the company's history.

Below: Pfizer's Zithromax, an innovative macrolide antibiotic, is ideal for parents of young children, like the little girl shown here with her Zithromax zebra, because it is a once-daily, short-course medication.

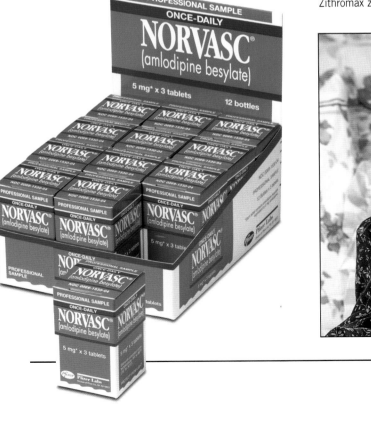

Above: Fred Telling, right, seen here with Corporate Employee Resources Executive Vice President William "B.J." Robison, heads Pfizer's Corporate Strategic Planning and Policy unit. Telling's mission is to strengthen Pfizer's ability to anticipate and influence global regulatory and competitive trends and to provide strategies that will enable Pfizer to deliver exceptional operating performance.

Above right: As senior vice president, Worldwide Marketing, Pfizer Pharmaceuticals Group, Pat Kelly's responsibilities include directing multidisciplinary teams in the development and application of products and services for the management of cardiovascular, central nervous system, and respiratory disorders, infectious diseases, diabetes, and arthritis. A variety of disease management programs, which provide materials like those shown here, help doctors and patients manage chronic diseases.

Right: As the company has grown in size, financial risk management has become more critical. Pfizer Treasurer Alan Levin, who joined the Controllers Division in 1987, stays focused on identifying new opportunities and solutions to the financial risks of managing a global organization.

Pfizer immediately filed a patent application, which was awarded to Bright. However, when the company learned that Pliva Pharmaceuticals in Yugoslavia had filed an identical application a month earlier, it voluntarily rescinded its patent and became a business partner with Pliva. The resulting drug, Zithromax, differs from other antibiotics by leaving the bloodstream and lodging in infected tissue for a long time, which means that an effective dose can be very low. This is a major reason the drug works so well for pediatric patients.

Mike Bright notes that another plus is the drug's ability to treat sexually transmitted diseases like chlamydia and gonorrhea. As he puts it, "The Food and Drug Administration gave us a clear signal that our compound is the indicated drug for these diseases."

Appropriately, these three blockbuster drugs illuminated the final years of service for two of Pfizer's extraordinary leaders. In 1991, Pfizer President Gerald Laubach announced that he was stepping down, capping a 40-year career that had led Pfizer science into the modern age. Laubach was one of only a handful of U.S. corporate leaders who had successfully bridged the worlds of science, top management, and public policy. His vision and practical skills had played a key role in building the superior organizations in research, development, and marketing that had given Pfizer the most promising pipeline in its history.

Shortly afterward, Edmund T. Pratt, Jr., announced that he would retire within a year. He had personally led the fight to protect the company's intellectual property. As a Harvard Business School professor put it, "Under the leadership of Chairman and CEO Edmund Pratt, Pfizer was instrumental in transforming intellectual property from a lawyer's specialty into an international trade issue of great concern to governments around the world."

After these two leaders retired, the board decided to consolidate Pfizer's two top positions. The man they elected to take Pfizer into the next millennium was William C. Steere, Jr., then president of Pfizer Pharmaceuticals. In 1990, Steere was named president, and in 1991, he became CEO, and the following year, he was elected chairman of the board.

Steere became Pfizer's eleventh CEO at a promising yet perilous time for the industry and the company. He inherited a prosperous enterprise with sales of pharmaceuticals — including medicines for humans and animals as well as self-medication products — generating nearly $4 billion a year. However, the pharmaceutical industry was again coming under attack. The administration of President Clinton was intent on exerting greater control over America's health care system in a way that could have a major negative impact on the research-based pharmaceutical industry.

Responding to changing market forces, many of the leading drug companies cut their sales forces, bought distribution outlets, or merged with other companies. Steere, however, marched to the beat of a different drum. Confident that Pfizer already stood on the high ground, he focused the company on its core competencies, trimmed fat, streamlined operations, invested more in R&D, expanded Pfizer's sales and marketing force, and prepared the company for what would be the most successful decade in its history.

At the close of 1990, current and future leaders posed for this group portrait. From back row left, clockwise: Edward Bessey, executive vice president; Bill Steere, president-elect, Pfizer Inc; Jean-Paul Vallès, executive vice president; Ed Pratt, chairman and CEO; and Pfizer President Gerald Laubach.

Chairman of the Board and Chief Executive Officer William C. Steere, Jr., has propelled Pfizer to the top of the pharmaceutical industry.

CHAPTER FOURTEEN

PFIZER IN FOCUS: THE STEERE YEARS

At Pfizer, innovation is not the sole province of research. It permeates everything we do, from the discovery process to product distribution. In marketing and manufacturing and finance and legal and information technology, as well as in all the line and staff groups, we've adopted innovative strategies.

— William C. Steere, Jr., 1997

EARLY IN THE 1990s, WILLIAM C. Steere, Jr., took the helm as Pfizer's chairman and CEO. A man of vision and intellectual acuity, he was convinced that Pfizer had the potential to become the world's premier pharmaceutical company, and he designed a strategy to achieve that goal.

Steere believed that Pfizer's greatest strength lay in its ability to discover, develop, and market innovative pharmaceuticals. His goal was to focus on that strength and build on the values that have sustained the company throughout its long history — integrity, respect for people, customer focus, performance, innovation, leadership, teamwork, and community. In less than a decade, this strategy has brought Pfizer the greatest success it has ever known.

Like many of his predecessors, Pfizer's eleventh CEO often swam against the tide. When a host of high-profile mergers reshaped the industry, Pfizer stayed the course, preserving its independence. When competitors reduced their R&D budgets, Pfizer dramatically expanded its investments. When others cut their field forces, Pfizer greatly increased the number of its sales representatives. Bill Steere recognized the key role the field force plays in the transfer of technology between the company's research laboratories and the practicing physician.

Over the course of the decade that began with his election as CEO in 1991 and chairman of the board in 1992, Pfizer pared away nine businesses that either were unrelated to health care or did not meet the corporation's financial requirements. These businesses included all the units of the Specialty Minerals and Food Sciences divisions, as well as consumer products segments such as Coty perfumes and beauty products.

Henry A. McKinnell, Jr., who was vice president of Corporate Strategic Planning during early debates that led to the refocusing of Pfizer in the 1990s, explains: "What we were debating was not the attractiveness of Specialty Minerals or Food Sciences, but how we wanted to position Pfizer in the 1990s. The concern with the future of pharmaceuticals in the 1960s and 1970s led us to pursue a strategy of deliberate diversification. During the 1990s, we chose to focus on our core strengths. No one was a more staunch advocate of our need to refocus than Bill Steere."

In 1998, the sale of four other businesses, all in the Medical Technology Group — Valleylab (electro-surgical devices), American Medical Systems (impo-

Pfizer unveiled a special commemorative logo to celebrate its 150th anniversary in 1999.

tence and incontinence implants), Howmedica (orthopedic devices), and Schneider Worldwide (devices for international cardiology and radiology applications) — completed Pfizer's transformation from a company of diverse, unrelated businesses into one focused exclusively on medicines for people and animals.

Research: The First Key to Success

One of Pfizer's hallmarks in the 1990s has been its extraordinary commitment to R&D. The company recognized that in the fiercely competitive pharmaceutical market, the first key to success was an R&D operation that could generate promising new drug candidates across a wide range of disease categories. In 1991, Pfizer invested almost $757 million in research. Just eight years later, that sum had more than tripled to $2.8 billion, one of the largest amounts invested in R&D by any pharmaceutical company in the world.

Pfizer's Central Research division, which had been created only two decades earlier, in 1971, had been put on track to become a research powerhouse by its first leader, Dr. Barry Bloom.

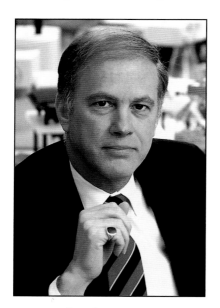

His successors, Dr. John Niblack and Dr. George Milne, built on this accomplishment. They transformed Pfizer's research operation into a nimble, globally integrated organization and helped erase the lines that typically separate R&D from marketing.

Both Niblack, who heads Pfizer's worldwide research efforts, and Milne, who heads Pfizer's Central Research division, have refined and accelerated the company's discovery and development process. Today, using the most advanced technologies available, Pfizer scientists maintain a discovery program of unprecedented breadth. Their search for new treatments extends to more than 100 projects in 18 major

Above: John Niblack joined Pfizer as a molecular biologist in 1967. He rose to become the company's executive vice president in 1997, responsible for the Central Research, Animal Health, Licensing and Development, and Quality Control divisions. He became vice chairman of the board in 1999.

Left: George Milne, who has been president of Central Research since 1993, anticipates an explosion in biomedical insights and the tools of innovation as we enter the next century.

disease groups, a therapeutic agenda that is made possible by the high productivity of Pfizer's discovery scientists.

As Dr. Niblack told Pfizer shareholders at the 1999 annual meeting, "The combination of new drug target insights gained through molecular genetic research with high-speed synthesis and robotic, very-high-throughput screening will lead to the pipeline that will fuel Pfizer's growth into the 21st century."

The strength of currently marketed products provides a firm foundation for that growth. In the past ten years, the company has launched 11 major products — six in the last three years alone. Pfizer's scientists, more than 7,000 strong

Above: Pfizer executives welcome shareholders at the company's annual meeting in 1993. From left: William C. Steere, Jr., chairman and CEO; Henry A. McKinnell, Jr., now president and chief operating officer; and C.L. Clemente, now executive vice president, Corporate Affairs.

Below right: Ken Bowler, right, who heads Pfizer's Washington, D.C., office as vice president, Federal Government Relations, welcomes New York Congressman Charles Rangel to an issues forum held at Pfizer World Headquarters in 1998.

worldwide, have made a record number of new discoveries, generating more new products than ever before in Pfizer's history. Recognized as the industry leader in R&D, Pfizer is currently expanding all three of its major research centers — in the United States, England, and Japan — adding more than one million square feet and doubling current capacity.

The Bridge to the Market

Having led the U.S. Pharmaceuticals Group before becoming president of Pfizer, Bill Steere understood the critical role played by the domestic and international sales and marketing groups. Early on, he and other senior managers recognized that unifying the two groups would be in the best interests of the company. Even more important,

they realized that it would enable Pfizer to better serve patients worldwide. At the end of 1996, the company initiated a major reorganization of its pharmaceutical business. This restructuring was calculated to abolish whatever remained of the wall between domestic and international operations.

The new global entity took shape as the Pfizer Pharmaceuticals Group (PPG). Announcing the reorganization, Henry McKinnell, the newly appointed president of PPG, described its advantages:

Through a global business perspective, the Pfizer Pharmaceuticals Group will be structured to focus closely on our customers and to bring new medicines to patients to meet unmet medical needs. The new PPG will also enhance our global effectiveness while maintaining the unwavering concentration of individual country operations on their markets.

The reconfigured organization streamlined its operations, enabling it to serve patients and providers throughout the world faster, better, and more economically. Karen Katen, president, U.S. Pharmaceuticals, and executive vice president, Pfizer Pharmaceuticals Group, whose experience and savvy have made Pfizer's marketing and sales the envy of the industry, stressed that integration and cooperation would benefit everyone in the company's sales and marketing groups:

We are all actively involved in the study and development of the same products. They're in different markets, and you have different customers, different players, but the products are a constant. So, even though a physician in France will say he doesn't practice medicine like a physician in Germany, the same could be said about Boston and Dallas. I think what we will be able to do with the new global organization is really help each other.

The new organization's integrated operations and intensified focus quickly bore fruit. During 1997 and 1998, its first two years as a consolidated entity, the Pfizer Pharmaceuticals Group outpaced all its competitors in new-prescription growth around the world. With major investments in R&D, sales, and marketing, Pfizer's worldwide sales in 1998 grew at a faster rate than those of any of the ten largest pharmaceutical companies and at about three times the rate of the industry as a whole.

To do justice to Pfizer's unprecedented number of products, the company began to steadily expand its field forces. In 1990, Pfizer inaugurated Pratt Pharmaceuticals, a new field force named in honor of Chairman Edmund T. Pratt, Jr. In 1997, it launched Powers Rx, named for former Chairman

THE GENETIC REVOLUTION

WHEN NEWS OF THE BIOMEDICAL revolution in genetics first began to trickle out of labs and into the mainstream media in the 1970s, its potential and risks were immediately topics of widespread debate. Toward the middle of the 1990s, science fiction movies depicted fantastic risks associated with genetic manipulation, most notably in the blockbuster film *Jurassic Park*.

Scientists, however, were focused on the incredible benefits that would accrue to medicine if a way could be found to correct flaws in the billions of bits of DNA that exist in every cell. The potential of the genetic revolution lay in the ability of researchers to map and identify single genes and to develop techniques to clone those genes, because once a gene had been cloned, it could be placed in a host organism or cell and replicated indefinitely. The implications of such an achievement were breathtaking.

But genetic engineering also is a practical exploration of a new discipline. While other drug companies prepared themselves as quickly as possible to explore this new discipline and sought ways to produce human hormones and other large-protein molecules, Pfizer cautiously appraised the situation. John Niblack, the company's chief scientist, was part of the team that elected to carefully control Pfizer's entry into biotechnology. Niblack explained:

There was a tremendous amount of faddism that was difficult to resist, but we did.

Pfizer was one of the first companies to establish an automated gene sequencing laboratory, which was located at its Groton site.

Jack Powers, and the following year, Pfizer inaugurated Alta Pharmaceuticals. By 1999, the company's worldwide field forces numbered nearly 18,000. In only four years, they had almost doubled in size. In March 1999, in a fitting tribute to the man whose support had been critical to the growth of Pfizer's field forces, the company launched Steere Pharmaceuticals.

Recognizing that the success of the field force depends on more than its numbers, Pfizer has championed innovations that continue to set it apart from its competitors. An outstanding training program, the latest technological advances, a resilient organizational structure, dynamic marketplace strategies, and matrix management enable Pfizer's field forces to respond quickly and effectively to an astonishing range of conditions across different geographical areas. Using principles drawn from matrix management, Pfizer's sales forces respond immediately to individuals and institutions, as well as to changes in local health care markets.

The effectiveness of Pfizer's pharmaceutical sales forces was underscored in 1999, when, for the fourth year in a row, U.S. physicians ranked them number one overall.

Molecular genetics became possible in the 1980s. Scientists could take a gene for a natural hormone, like insulin or growth hormone, and clone it, and put it in a microorganism and ferment the microorganism so that they were able to produce the hormone. This didn't interest us very much because we felt that the number of such hormonal targets was small and that it was not an important area for meeting medical needs or for large commercial opportunities.

Instead, Pfizer approached the science from a different angle. According to Richard Hinman, who directed work on gene science at Pfizer in the 1970s:

We did a slow waltz up to the subject. We got into the business and started building the group, and we had several different projects. We kept building the group on the assumption that we were going to find something.

What they found was a perfect discovery tool. Scientists and executives conjectured that cloning would allow production of large amounts of rare and difficult-to-obtain human receptors. Those receptors could then be used by research teams for testing in disease models. For instance, a team might expect a drug to react with a certain neuroreceptor in a particular way. Developing this drug and testing it in humans, where the receptor resides, can be both expensive and time consuming. Instead, the receptor itself is spliced into a microorganism, which is then fermented to produce large quantities, and suddenly the team has access to as much test material as it needs.

"We slowly built a very effective group that is well targeted today," says Alan Proctor, vice president, Discovery Genomic Targets and Cancer Research. "We now have a credible capability in the area, not the largest in the industry, but perhaps the best focused. In the last few years, our Molecular Genetics and Protein Chemistry Department has gone from the smallest to the largest department of the Discovery operation."

Interestingly, Pfizer's entry into molecular biology recalled one of the company's oldest strengths: fermentation. The accepted way of producing a desired gene or molecule is to splice it into a microorganism and then grow that organism in fermentation tanks, just as James Currie had fermented citric acid many decades earlier. "The discipline of biotechnology will be a very important part of Pfizer's next century, as it was of Pfizer's first century. It's stimulating being both at the cutting edge of research and yet also part of that long-standing continuum," says Ken Taksen, executive director of Bioprocess R&D.

Taking the Pharmaceutical World by Storm

The 11 products that Pfizer introduced between 1989 and 1999 have driven the company's unprecedented success in the 1990s. Innovative and targeted to satisfy unmet medical needs, most of these products are leading medicines in their therapeutic class. Pfizer's best-selling drug, Norvasc, for example, is the world's number one antihypertensive. Diflucan is the world's leading prescription antifungal. Zoloft is the globe's second-largest-selling antidepressant. Zithromax is the most prescribed brand-name oral antibiotic in the United States, and Viagra, a revolutionary drug for erectile dysfunction, has been not only a phenomenally successful medicine, but also a worldwide cultural phenomenon.

The FDA approved Viagra at the end of March 1998, and the drug hit the market the following month. Almost overnight, its sensational success transformed Pfizer into one of the world's most-

recognized pharmaceutical companies. As Bill Steere observed at the Viagra launch on May 5, 1998, "Never in Pfizer's history has any product generated such interest from the public, the media, and the medical community."

Within weeks, *The Wall Street Journal* was hailing Viagra as "one of the fastest-selling drugs in the history of medicine." A media sensation, Viagra was featured on the covers of *Time*, *Newsweek*, and *Business Week*, as well as on national television programs such as "20/20," "Nightline," and "Dateline NBC."

In a typical month in 1998, doctors wrote some 800,000 prescriptions for Viagra. After a year, one out of every three doctors in America had prescribed Viagra, and by the beginning of 1999, Pfizer had introduced the drug in more than 50 countries.

Becoming the Partner of Choice

Pfizer has had a long history of great innovations, but it recognizes that no single company has a monopoly on good ideas. To build on and

Above: In 1997, Pfizer joined forces with Eisai of Japan to copromote Eisai's Aricept, a milestone treatment for Alzheimer's disease. Attending the rollout ceremonies were, from left, Soichi Matsuno, president, Eisai North America; Bill Steere, Pfizer chairman and CEO; Karen Katen, president, U.S. Pharmaceuticals; Haruo Naito, president and CEO, Eisai Co., Ltd.; and Hank McKinnell, president, Pfizer Pharmaceuticals Group.

Left: Following the launch of Viagra, former U.S. Senator Bob Dole partnered with Pfizer to educate men about erectile dysfunction, a significantly misunderstood and undertreated condition. This ad appeared in February 1999 in *The New York Times*.

BUILDING A NETWORK OF STRATEGIC ALLIANCES

PFIZER CONTINUALLY SEEKS PARTNERS, such as those shown in the figure above, that are similarly committed to innovation.

The company's many alliances form a strategic network intended to strengthen Pfizer's work in discovery and development. Through these partnerships the company has gained access to the most sophisticated molecular science to help it identify genes and determine their function. All of these collaborations have the same purpose — to discover and develop innovative medicines more quickly and to help more people worldwide.

"We at Pfizer," says Central Research President George Milne, "have committed ourselves to becoming the partner of choice, enabling us to enter quality liaisons. We seek partners that recognize the realities of our business and who are willing to work with us to create the paradigm shifts that enable both of us to share in a product's market success — success that will increase as the health care environment of the future becomes even more favorable. In so doing, we strive to create a win-win situation for our partners, ourselves, and, most importantly, for patients. This is the basis for any successful venture."

Lambert's cholesterol-lowering medicine; and Aricept, Eisai's Alzheimer's drug. Most recently, Pfizer joined with Inhale Therapeutic Systems, Inc., and Hoechst Marion Roussel AG to develop an inhalable form of insulin.

Serving Consumers over the Counter

Pfizer's wide array of consumer health care products complements the company's prescription pharmaceuticals. These products help meet the growing need worldwide for over-the-counter medications to treat life's minor, but often chronic, ailments and discomforts. Pfizer's over-the-counter remedies include eye care treatments, anti-itch medicines, sleep aids, pediculicides, analgesics, and skin care products. A number of these products are household names — BenGay, Cortizone, Desitin, RID, Unisom, and Visine.

With the trend toward self-medication growing stronger each day, Pfizer aims to further serve consumers by making more of its pharmaceutical products available over the counter. OTC products such as Reactine, an antihistamine for allergies available in Canada, and Diflucan One, a single-pill treatment for vaginal yeast infections that is marketed in the United Kingdom, enable consumers to take even greater charge of their own health. This strategy also allows Pfizer to extend the commercial life of a pharmaceutical well beyond its patent expiration.

complement its strengths, Pfizer actively seeks out alliances. Such collaborations include partnerships, copromotions, and licensing agreements with individuals, companies, and universities around the world. Pfizer's prowess in R&D, sales, medical, and marketing has also made it a partner of choice for a growing number of companies. As a result, Pfizer is today copromoting Celebrex, an important new arthritis drug discovered and developed by Monsanto's G.D. Searle Division; Lipitor, Warner

Above: Underscoring the company's commitment to employee civic participation, Pfizer's Capitol Days program gives U.S. field forces the opportunity to see state governments in action. Here, Chuck Hardwick, left, vice president, State Government Relations, and Forest Harper, vice president of Sales, center, Roerig, meet Texas Governor George W. Bush in Austin.

Center: Alex L. Bachmann, who leads the Consumer Health Care Group, has had extensive experience in Europe and Latin America over the course of his 27-year career at Pfizer.

Right: An array of Consumer Health Care products, which includes U.S. market leaders BenGay, Cortizone, Desitin, RID, Unisom, and Visine.

MICROBES: A TRAVELING EXHIBIT

TO PROVE THAT LEARNING ABOUT germs can be fun, Pfizer, one of the world's great pioneers in microbial research, is sponsoring an interactive traveling exhibit, "Microbes: Invisible Invaders … Amazing Allies." The exhibit premiered at the Ontario Science Centre in Toronto, Canada, in 1997. It made its U.S. debut at the Liberty Science Center in New Jersey in 1998, and opened at the Smithsonian's Ripley Center in Washington, D.C., in 1999. In all, the exhibit will travel to 13 U.S. cities between 1999 and 2003.

To create a multimedia microbial wonderland, a Pfizer team worked for two years with BBH Exhibits and the National Institutes of Health. The exhibit's designers used some of today's most advanced technology — 3-D animation, computer graphics, virtual reality, and video games — to depict the history of microbial science and its effects on humanity. Visitors wend their way through 13 different exhibits, including a skull-lined 14th century crypt in plague-devastated Paris, a kitchen filled with talking cartoon microbes, and a room in which hologram screens project stunning 3-D images of viruses.

Underscoring the connection between Pfizer's pioneering efforts in microbial science and its sponsorship of the exhibit, Lou Clemente, executive vice president, Corporate Affairs, noted that "Pfizer has been in the forefront of developing ways to put microbes to good use for almost 150 years. Pfizer led the way in the fermentation of citric acid and then, in the 1940s, pioneered the mass production of the wonder drug penicillin, which in many ways launched the age of modern pharmaceuticals."

The exhibit's Microbial Universe is a blacklighted environment of 3-D holograms, robotic models, and interactive displays.

Innovation in Animal Health

Pfizer's intense focus on innovative pharmaceuticals applies as much to its Animal Health Group as to its human pharmaceuticals unit. To build on the company's strength in medicines for livestock, Pfizer began looking, early in the decade, for an acquisition that would give it a competitive presence in the growing companion animal, or pet, marketplace. SmithKline Beecham's animal health group fit the bill perfectly, and in 1995, Pfizer acquired this unit for $1.45 billion. This acquisition, the largest in the company's history, made Pfizer one of the world's leading producers of medicines for animals, with a pharmaceutical portfolio of anti-infectives, antiparasitics, anti-inflammatories, vaccines, and other remedies for more than 30 species in over 140 countries.

Brian Barrett, president of the Animal Health Group, has deftly guided the melding of the Pfizer and SmithKline Beecham animal health businesses. Pfizer's Animal Health Group now has the greatest range of innovative animal health products in the company's history. Propelling the division's growth today are premier products like the livestock endectocide Dectomax, the canine anti-arthritic Rimadyl, the swine vaccine RespiSure, and Anipryl, the first approved treatment for canine Cushing's disease and canine cognitive disorder.

Few other Pfizer Animal Health products, however, have generated as much excitement as the division's new blockbuster, Revolution (Stronghold in some markets). Introduced in August 1999, Revolution is an innovative, safe, easy-to-use pet product that protects dogs and cats from heartworms, fleas, and other harmful parasites with just a spot a month in front of the shoulder blades.

The Rewards of Focus

By the mid-1990s, Pfizer's focus on pharmaceuticals had begun to pay handsome dividends. Company revenues increased from $4 billion in 1991 to more than $13.5 billion in 1998. During these years, the value of Pfizer's stock grew almost tenfold. Return on the company's stock far outpaced the average rate of return for both the Standard & Poor's 500 Composite Stock Index and the Peer Group Index. In fact, during the years that Bill Steere has been CEO, Pfizer's stock has split four times — two-for-one three times and three-for-one in June 1999.

Not surprisingly, the business press has been quick to trumpet Pfizer's stellar performance. In 1996, *Business Week* named Steere one of the "Top 25 Managers of the Year." In 1997 and 1998, in its annual survey, *Fortune* named Pfizer the world's most admired pharmaceutical company. And in 1999, *Forbes* named Pfizer "Company of the Year."

The Changing Face of Health Care

Pfizer's progress during the 1990s was remarkable by any measure, but it was all the more impressive in view of the tremendous changes in the health care market worldwide. In the United States, this issue came to the fore early in the 1990s, when the new Clinton administration set out to radically change how health care was delivered in America.

Industry detractors denounced the so-called "excessive" profits generated by pharmaceutical companies, ignoring the fact that it typically costs more than $500 million to bring even one new drug to market.

Above: Brian Barrett, pictured with his friend Jake, heads Pfizer's Animal Health Group, one of the world's leading producers of medicines for animals.

Below: The combined service of the Pfizer Pharmaceuticals Group's four area presidents totals an astonishing 109 years. Their extensive experience helps them guide the success of Pfizer's operations in important world markets. From left: Mohand Sidi Said, who is responsible for the Asia, Africa, and Middle East regions; Hugh O'Connor, who leads Pfizer Europe; Ian Read, who manages operations in Canada and Latin America; and Karen Katen, who is responsible for the United States.

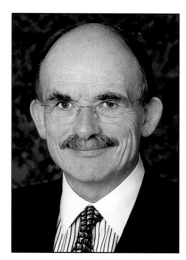

Industry critics also refused to recognize the tremendous risks involved in discovering and developing a new drug. From millions of screening tests, only 1,000 compounds may show promise. Of those, perhaps 15 actually become candidates for development. Only one of these 15 is likely to make it to market, a journey that usually takes an additional 10 to 15 years, leaving pharmaceutical companies little patent-protected time in which to recoup their investment in order to fund future research. The industry's critics also ignored the fact that convenient, cost-effective pharmaceuticals save countless lives and dollars.

The industry had never encountered such a barrage of criticism. Public policy challenges, price pressures, and mandatory rebates combined to threaten its ability to discover, develop, and deliver innovative medicines to help people live healthier and fuller lives. At the same time, market forces were driving major changes in the delivery of health care, with intense cost pressures accelerating the expansion of managed-care organizations. In response, several pharmaceutical companies spent huge sums to vertically integrate by buying pharmacy benefit management companies (PBMs).

When such acquisitions became the rage, many warned that Pfizer would be left behind if it failed to buy a PBM. Focusing on Pfizer's identity and core strengths, the company refused to be swayed.

The Pfizer Foundation's support for Oklahoma State University's Center for Science Literacy exemplifies the company's commitment to academia and the sciences. Here, Pfizer Labs Regional Manager Jo Anne Harper presents a check to Governor Frank Keating, right, and Oklahoma State University President James Halligan during a press conference at the state capitol in June 1999.

Below: In March 1999, Pfizer launched its sixth primary U.S. sales force, Steere Pharmaceuticals, named in honor of its chief executive officer and chairman of the board. During Bill Steere's tenure, Pfizer has built the most productive and best-respected sales force in the industry.

Primed for Greater Success

Resisting prevalent trends helped prime the company for greater success. Relying on a long-term strategy that played to its strengths, the company set an ambitious goal. In 1997, Pfizer announced that it would aim to become the number one pharmaceutical company in the world in 2001. Pfizer intended to achieve this goal by doing what it does best: discovering, developing, and bringing to market innovative medicines that cure disease and improve the quality of patients' lives. At the same time, the company reaffirmed its commitment to its eight core values: integrity, respect for people, customer focus, performance, innovation, leadership, teamwork, and community.

Giving Back to the Community

For Pfizer and its people, doing the right thing has always meant helping others. Today, the company supports a wide range of philanthropic programs that include relief efforts to aid the victims of natural disasters, educational initiatives to help young people, and exemplary medical programs like Sharing the Care. This program, launched in 1993, provides Pfizer medicines free of charge to many uninsured Americans whose income falls below the poverty line. Working through a nationwide network of more than 350 community health care clinics, Pfizer has, in the last six years, filled nearly three million prescriptions, donating medicines valued at nearly $180 million and benefiting more than a million patients.

In late 1998, Pfizer launched its most ambitious international philanthropic initiative — a $66 million public health program to help eliminate trachoma, the world's leading cause of preventable blindness, in five developing countries — Mali, Morocco, Ghana, Tanzania, and Vietnam. Central to this campaign is Pfizer's long-acting antibiotic Zithromax. A single dose of this innovative drug is far more efficient, cost-effective, and convenient than the alternative treatment for trachoma — an antibiotic ointment that must be applied topically twice a day for six weeks.

As important as the donation of Zithromax is, the company's effort does not stop there. Recognizing that trachoma is often caused by lack of hygiene and the use of nonpotable water, Pfizer is simultaneously supporting a public health strategy

CORPORATE GOVERNANCE

IN THE EARLY 1970s, PFIZER'S BOARD OF directors began to distinguish itself from the typical corporate board. Recognizing that the boards of the future would be comprised mostly of outside directors, Chairman Jack Powers asked New York financier Felix Rohatyn to become Pfizer's first outside director. Rohatyn was followed by John Opal, then chairman of IBM.

Terence Gallagher, Pfizer's first vice president of Corporate Governance, observes:

Outside board members in that era were usually known to the chairman, and were chosen by him. As we moved into the Steere era, our large institutional shareholders liked to see new directors chosen by a board committee or by the board itself. Bill Steere carried on Ed Pratt's tradition of maintaining an independent board, and he created the Corporate Governance Department.

Led by Bill Steere, Pfizer's board today is a blend of talents. As Gallagher points out:

Our board has something very substantial to offer to the company, whether in science, finance, or general business. This is a group of people who take the job seriously, do their homework, and are not averse to raising tough questions — and on infrequent occasions, even voting against management.

Today, Pfizer's 15-member board of directors is comprised of 12 outside directors and its three top executives: Bill Steere, chairman of the board and CEO; Henry McKinnell, Ph.D., president and chief operating officer, and president, Pfizer Pharmaceuticals Group; and John Niblack, Ph.D., vice chairman of the board.

One of the outside directors, Jean-Paul Vallès, Ph.D., a former Pfizer vice chairman and now chairman and CEO of Mineral Technologies Inc., has been a Pfizer board member since 1980.

The outside members of the Pfizer board (in alphabetical order):

In Morocco, U.S. First Lady Hillary Rodham Clinton talks with Michael Hodin, vice president, Corporate Affairs, left, about Pfizer's initiative to battle trachoma, the world's leading cause of preventable blindness. Pfizer is donating millions of doses of its antibiotic Zithromax to combat trachoma in Morocco as well as in four other developing nations.

called SAFE (surgery, antibiotics, face washing, and environmental change) to help improve conditions at the community level.

At Pfizer, reaching out to help others is a long-standing tradition — whether it is next door or half a world away. Company employees volunteer for a host of community programs, and their per capita contributions to America's annual United Way drive, matched dollar-for-dollar by the company, place them firmly in the ranks of America's most generous people.

Pfizer's philanthropic activities not only burnish its reputation and demonstrate its commitment to helping others; they also add to shareholder value by improving the company's standing with customers, as well as with regulatory and legislative authorities. For example, Pfizer's support for a whole array of projects in

Michael S. Brown, M.D., regental professor, University of Texas Southwestern Medical Center; distinguished chair, biomedical sciences; and Nobel laureate

M. Anthony Burns, chairman, president, and CEO, Ryder System, Inc.

W. Don Cornwell, chairman and CEO, Granite Broadcasting Corporation

George B. Harvey, former chairman, president, and CEO, Pitney Bowes, Inc.

Constance J. Horner, guest scholar, The Brookings Institution; former assistant to the President of the United States

Stanley O. Ikenberry, Ph.D., president, American Council on Education

Harry P. Kamen, former chairman, president, and CEO, Metropolitan Life Insurance Company

Thomas G. Labrecque, former president, The Chase Manhattan Corporation and The Chase Manhattan Bank

Dana G. Mead, Ph.D., chairman and CEO, Tenneco, Inc.

Franklin D. Raines, chairman and CEO, Fannie Mae

Ruth J. Simmons, Ph.D., president, Smith College

Jean-Paul Vallès, Ph.D., chairman, Minerals Technologies Inc.

Bill Steere's state-of-the-business address highlighted the company's celebration of its mission, vision, and values at New York City's Lincoln Center in 1998. In September 1999, several thousand metropolitan area employees returned to Lincoln Center to celebrate Pfizer's 150th anniversary, a milestone event shared by their colleagues around the world via live broadcast.

Above: Hank McKinnell began his Pfizer career in Tokyo nearly three decades ago. Appointed Pfizer's president and chief operating officer in 1999, he also heads the company's principal operating division, the Pfizer Pharmaceuticals Group.

Right: Karen Katen, who has driven Pfizer's U.S. Pharmaceuticals operations to new heights, was named one of the 50 most powerful women in American business by *Fortune* magazine in 1998. She has been with the company for 25 years.

Below: Chief Financial Officer David Shedlarz, a 23-year veteran, re-engineered Pfizer's financial operations, a bold step that has led to innovations throughout the organization.

Brooklyn has benefited the company enormously.

A few years ago, when most other businesses abandoned the Williamsburg section of Brooklyn, Pfizer decided to stay. By operating its plant 24 hours a day, the company helped keep crucial jobs in the community. Pfizer also began a redevelopment program — revitalizing the

neighborhood around the plant and working to improve safety, housing, education, and commercial development. In addition, the company converted one of its buildings into a kind of charter elementary school — which has achieved outstanding results.

The Next Chapter

Today, a new generation of leaders is preparing to take Pfizer into the next century. As the 1990s come to a close, succession planning is in full swing. In May 1999, Pfizer's board of directors elected Dr. Henry McKinnell, executive vice president, Pfizer Inc, and president of the Pfizer Pharmaceuticals Group, the company's new president and chief operating officer. The directors simultaneously named Dr. John Niblack, executive vice president of Pfizer Inc, the company's new vice chairman. In addition, Lou Clemente, senior vice president, Corporate Affairs; Paul S. Miller, senior vice president and general counsel; William "B.J." Robison, senior vice president, Corporate Employee Resources; and David Shedlarz, senior vice president and chief financial officer, were named executive vice presidents of Pfizer Inc.

The board also elected Karen Katen, vice president, Pfizer Inc, executive vice president, Pfizer Pharmaceuticals Group, and president, U.S.

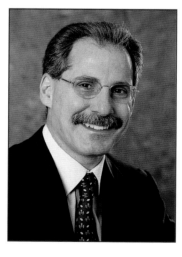

Pharmaceuticals; and Dr. George Milne, vice president, Pfizer Inc, and president, Central Research, to positions as senior vice presidents of the company.

Looking back over Pfizer's 150-year history, it is clear that the company's values have been the determining factor in its success. It is equally clear that Pfizer employees continue to put those values into practice.

Today, the men and women of Pfizer are writing the next chapter in an extraordinary story that

In 1993, the three men who have led Pfizer for the past 34 years — former chairmen John J. Powers, Jr., left; Edmund T. Pratt, Jr., right; and current chairman William C. Steere, Jr., center — came together to honor Barry Bloom, retiring head of Central Research.

began a century and a half ago. When Charles Pfizer and Charles Erhart purchased a red brick building in Brooklyn, they gave birth to an enterprise that today circles the globe. By marshaling the powers of innovation and enterprise, successive generations of Pfizer people have pushed back the frontiers of science, pioneering innovative treatments and cures. The fine-chemicals company founded in 1849 is today a research-driven pharmaceutical powerhouse in the vanguard of modern medicine.

Throughout its history, Pfizer has been unequivocally committed to research and innovation. The same ingenuity that drove its founders to make and market a palatable cure for intestinal parasites later inspired Pfizer scientists to break new ground in fermentation technology and develop a way to manufacture citric acid from sugar. That same questing spirit made Pfizer a pioneer in the "Age of Antibiotics," the first company to successfully mass-produce penicillin and the first to bring the world wonder drugs like streptomycin, Terramycin, and Tetracyn.

Over the last 150 years, Pfizer has made an invaluable contribution to America and to the world. Millions of patients have been protected, cured, or saved by Pfizer drugs, and innumerable others have had their health and hope restored as a result of treatments pioneered by Pfizer.

The legend of Pfizer is a history of excellence, achievement, and innovation. It is also a history of meeting intellectual challenges, discovering scientific solutions, and providing medical cures. As outstanding as Pfizer's achievements have been in the last 150 years, its prospects today are even brighter. The greatness of Pfizer's past is exceeded only by the promise of its future.

PFIZER LEADERSHIP HAS remained remarkably consistent for a company that has been in business for 150 years. During Pfizer's first century, leadership was concentrated in the hands of just three families, the Pfizers, Erharts, and Andersons. These first generations of entrepreneurs transformed a small chemical manufacturer in Brooklyn known as Chas. Pfizer & Co. into the world's largest producer of penicillin.

Charles Pfizer
Cofounder

Charles Erhart
Cofounder

PFIZER'S GALLERY OF LEADERS
1849–1999

Recognizing that penicillin was only the beginning of a new era in medical breakthroughs, the next generation of leaders turned Pfizer into a formidable new pharmaceutical company, with a sales and marketing organization that circled the globe.

In recent years, Pfizer's leaders have focused the company on what it does best — discovering, developing, and bringing to market innovative medicines for humans and animals. Now at the dawn of the new millennium, with Chairman and CEO William C. Steere, Jr., at the helm, Pfizer is poised to become the world's premier research-based pharmaceutical company.

John J. Powers, Jr.
President (1965-1971)
Chief Executive Officer (1965-1972)
Chairman of the Board (1968-1972)

Gerald D. Laubach
President (1972-1991)

Emile Pfizer
President (1906-1941)
Chairman of the Board (1941)

John Anderson
Chairman of the Board (1914-1929)

William H. Erhart
Chairman of the Board (1929-1940)

George A. Anderson
President (1941-1945)
Chairman of the Board (1945-1949)

John L. Smith
President (1945-1949)
Chairman of the Board (1949-1950)

John E. McKeen
President (1949-1965)
Chairman of the Board (1950-1968)

Edmund T. Pratt, Jr.
President (1971-1972)
Chief Executive Officer (1972-1991)
Chairman of the Board (1972-1992)

Henry A. McKinnell, Jr.
President (1999-present)

William C. Steere, Jr.
President (1990-1991)
Chief Executive Officer (1991-present)
Chairman of the Board (1992-present)

BIBLIOGRAPHY

Books and Articles

"Antibiotic Feed Supplements Can Increase World Food Supplies." *Chemical and Engineering News* (January 28, 1952): 24.

"Artificial Citric Acid." *The Druggists Circular and Chemical Gazette*, Vol. XXXVIII (1894): 1.

"Bill Steere." *Pharmaceutical Executive*, Vol. 8, No. 11 (November 1988).

Blood Program in World War II. Medical Department, United States Army. Washington, DC: Office of the Surgeon General, Department of the Army, 1989.

"Calcium Blockers off to a Healthy Start." *The Wall Street Journal* (February 24, 1983): 1.

Cassidy, James H. *Medicine in America*. Baltimore, Maryland: The Johns Hopkins University Press, 1991.

"Colgate Will Buy Overseas Business of Plax Mouthwash." *The Wall Street Journal* (October 29, 1991): B6.

"Company of the Year." *MedAd News* (September 1995).

Cooper, John S., "Pfizer Success Story: Golf, Cologne and Other Unusual Gimmicks Boost Its Sales." *The Wall Street Journal* (June 4, 1954).

"Copy Chasers Select Chas. Pfizer & Co. As Company-of-the-Year." *Industrial Marketing Magazine* (January 1958): 147-152.

"Drug Firms Case to be Reviewed by Supreme Court." *The Wall Street Journal* (May 4, 1971): 2.

"Ed Pratt Elected President of Pfizer." *The Wall Street Journal* (September 24, 1971): 18.

"Eleven Scientists Will Seek Antibiotic Earth Molds." *New York Daily News* (May 16, 1951).

"Fair Exchange: Trade Talks Are Key for Many U.S. Firms, and They're Worried." *The Wall Street Journal* (December 3, 1991): A1.

"Feed Is Improved by Artificial Cows." *The New York Times* (April 11, 1954).

"Firm to Sell Two Businesses and Several Product Lines." *The Wall Street Journal* (June 24, 1991): C10.

"*Fortune* Publishes First-Ever Ranking of World's Most Admired Companies." *Fortune* magazine press release (October 7, 1997).

"Growth of Wonder Drugs." *Time* (October 1, 1951).

Halberstam, David. *The Fifties*. New York: Fawcett Columbine, 1993.

Handy, Bruce, "The Viagra Craze." *Time* (May 4, 1998): 54-55.

Harvard Business School. *Pfizer: Global Protection of Intellectual Property*. No. 9-392-073 (April 6, 1996): 6.

Hie gut Wurttemberg: Menschen, Geschichte und Landschaft unserer Heimat. (Translation) Supplement to *The Ludwigsburger Kreiszeitung*. April 17, 1959: pp. 19-20.

Hobby, Gladys L. *Penicillin: Meeting the Challenge*. New Haven, Connecticut: Yale University Press, 1985.

"How Pfizer Finds New Uses for Products." *Printers Ink Magazine* (January 23, 1959): 63-64.

"Il, Sil, Mine, Phyl." *The New Yorker* (July 14, 1956): 16.

"Karen Katen." *Pharmaceutical Executive*, Vol. 10, No. 4 (April 1990): 6.

Langreth, Robert, and Andrea Petersen, "Stampede Is on for the Impotence Pill." *The Wall Street Journal* (April 20, 1998): B1.

Lipin, Steven, "Stryker to Buy Pfizer Unit for $1.9 Billion." *The Wall Street Journal* (August 14, 1998): A3.

"Mark of Quality Set for Pfizer." *The New York Times* (April 18, 1972): 65.

McKeen, John, "The Chemically Trained Business Executive." *Chemical and Engineering News* (December 18, 1950): 4437.

Mines, Samuel. *Pfizer ... An Informal History*. New York: Pfizer Inc, 1978.

"Muscular Marketing." *Pharmaceutical Executive*, Vol. 17, No. 7 (July 1997): 3-4.

"The New Era of Lifestyle Drugs." *Business Week* (May 11, 1998): 96-97.

"Oral Research Laboratories to be Acquired Under Pact." *The Wall Street Journal* (August 23, 1988): 30.

Paludan, Phillip Shaw. *The Presidency of Abraham Lincoln*. Lawrence, Kansas: University Press of Kansas, 1994.

"Pfizer Acquires Mack Illertissen." *The Wall Street Journal* (October 25, 1972): 75.

"Pfizer Agrees to Buy Valleylab in a Stock Swap." *The Wall Street Journal* (November 12, 1982): 4.

"Pfizer Agrees to Sell Food-Science Group." *The Wall Street Journal* (December 15, 1995): B5.

"Pfizer Board Clears Sale of Stake in Unit, Repurchase of Shares." *The Wall Street Journal* (August 18, 1992): A12.

"Pfizer Is Cleared of Patent Fraud in Tetracycline Suit." *The Wall Street Journal* (August 21, 1980): 21.

"Pfizer Is Cleared to Market First Oral Form of Calcium Blockers, a New Heart Drug." *The Wall Street Journal* (January 5, 1982): 8.

"Pfizer Pays Cash to Acquire Radiologic Sciences Inc." *The Wall Street Journal* (December 7, 1976): 20.

"Pfizer Plans Purchase." *The Wall Street Journal* (September 8, 1986): 23.

"Pfizer Purchases Bain de Soleil Line from P&G, Looks for Other Acquisitions." *The Wall Street Journal* (August 16, 1995): B2.

"Pfizer Receives Approval of FDA to Market Drug." *The Wall Street Journal* (October 10, 1980): 33.

"Pfizer Stock Split." *The Wall Street Journal* (April 29, 1983): 42.

"Pfizer to Buy Animal-Health Business of SmithKline in $1.45 Billion Pact." *The Wall Street Journal* (November 25, 1994): A3.

"Pfizer to Hold Drug-Price Rise Under 3% in '93." *The Wall Street Journal* (January 26, 1993): B1.

"Pfizer to Invest More Than $115 Million in 4 Small Biotechnology Firms." *The Wall Street Journal* (March 24, 1995): B2.

"Pfizer's New Catch-up Tactics." *Business Week* (June 16, 1973): 63.

"Price Battle Follows on Heels of WPB Release of Penicillin." *Drug Trade News* (March 26, 1945): 1.

"Reporter at Large: Something Extraordinary." *The New Yorker* (July 28, 1951).

"Six Drug Makers Deny Charges of Fixing Prices in Antibiotics." *The New York Times* (August 3, 1958).

Smith, Geoffrey, "Steere the Course." *Industry Week* (June 3, 1996).

Steiner, Paul E. *Disease in the Civil War, Natural Biological Warfare in 1861-1865.* Springfield, Illinois: C.C. Thomas Publishing, 1968.

Sullivan, Mark. *Our Times.* ed. Dan Rather. (New York: Scribner, 1996).

"Summary of the F.T.C. Antibiotics Report." *The New York Times* (August 3, 1958).

Tannahill, Reay. *Food in History.* New York: Crown Trade Paperbacks, 1988.

Tanner, Ogden. *25 Years of Innovation: The Story of Pfizer Central Research.* Lyme, Connecticut: Greenwich Publishing Group, Inc., 1996.

Tindall, George, and David Shi. *America.* New York: W.W. Norton & Company, 1989.

"The Top Managers of 1995." *Business Week* (January 8, 1996): 58A.

"U.S. to Continue Probing Pfizer's Troubled Valve." *The Wall Street Journal* (February 27, 1990): 3.

Wiltse, Charles M. *Medical Service in the Mediterranean and Minor Theaters, United States in World War II.* Washington, DC: Office of the Chief of Military History, Department of the Army, 1965.

Pfizer Documents

A.A. Teeter to George Anderson, November 18, 1944, *Pfizer History Reference.* 5 vols., comp. George B. Stone. (New York: Pfizer Inc, 1977).

Annual Reports, 1950-1999

Board of Directors, Minutes, August 7, 1941.

Board of Directors Resolution, December 27, 1905.

F.E. Berquist to Charles Pfizer & Company, March 14, 1946, *Pfizer History Reference.* 5 vols., comp. George B. Stone. (New York: Pfizer Inc, 1977).

"Growth Through Innovation, A Brief Pfizer History." Booklet, Pfizer archives.

Jasper Kane to John L. Smith, October 13, 1941, *Pfizer History Reference.* 5 vols., comp. George B. Stone. (New York: Pfizer Inc, 1977).

Jasper Kane to John L. Smith, December 34, 1941, *Pfizer History Reference.* 5 vols., comp. George B. Stone. (New York: Pfizer Inc, 1977).

John Anderson to technical staff, March 16, 1932, *Pfizer History Reference.* 5 vols., comp. George B. Stone. (New York: Pfizer Inc, 1977).

John McKeen annual letter, January 31, 1963. Pfizer archives.

John McKeen annual letter, January 29, 1965. Pfizer archives.

John L. Smith annual letter, January 31, 1936, *Pfizer History Reference.* 5 vols., comp. George B. Stone. (New York: Pfizer Inc, 1977).

John L. Smith to Franklin Brehmer, January 31, 1931, *Pfizer History Reference.* 5 vols., comp. George B. Stone. (New York: Pfizer Inc, 1977).

John L. Smith to George Anderson, October 26, 1946, *Pfizer History Reference.* 5 vols., comp. George B. Stone. (New York: Pfizer Inc, 1977).

John L. Smith to John Anderson, December 1929, *Pfizer History Reference.* 5 vols., comp. George B. Stone. (New York: Pfizer Inc, 1977).

John L. Smith to plant staff, May 18, 1934, *Pfizer History Reference.* 5 vols., comp. George B. Stone. (New York: Pfizer Inc, 1977).

Laubach, Gerald. Remarks to Annual Meeting of Stockholders, April 23, 1981.

Laubach, Gerald. Response to Sen. Edward Kennedy's Questionnaire, June 21, 1974. Pfizer archives.

Maj. Gen. George Lull to Smith, July 4, 1944. *Pfizer History Reference.* 5 vols., comp. George B. Stone. (New York: Pfizer Inc, 1977).

"Manufacturing Creates a New Constellation." *Pfizer Scene,* Vol. 43. No. 3 (1996): 3-5.

"Mass Immunization — Big Blow to Polio." *Pfizer Scene* (August-September, 1964): 4-5.

McKeen, John. Invitation to Bid No. 33-017-48-1. August 25, 1947, *Pfizer History Reference.* 5 vols., comp. George B. Stone. (New York: Pfizer Inc, 1977).

McKeen, John. Speech to New York Society of Security Analysts, February 10, 1953. Pfizer archives.

McKeen, John. Statement Submitted to Subcommittee on Antitrust and Monopoly of the Senate Committee on the Judiciary Hearings on Antidiabetic Drugs. Pfizer archives.

McKinnell, Henry. Pfizer Employee's Day speech (July 23, 1998).

"Message From C.L. Clemente." *Pfizer Scene,* Vol. 44, No. 3 (1997): 5.

"Microbes." *Pfizer Scene,* Vol. 44, No. 3 (1997): 5.

"Pfizer Buys Interest in Maker in Plax." *Pfizer Scene* (July-August 1987): 11.

Pfizer History Reference. 5 vols., comp. George B. Stone. (New York: Pfizer Inc, 1977).

Pratt, Edward. "Pfizer: Bringing Science to Life." Speech to Newcomen Society (May 22, 1985).

"Protecting the Products of the Mind." *Pfizer Scene,* Vol. 42.3: 10-11.

R.G. Rhett to Charles Pfizer & Company, April 25, 1946, *Pfizer History Reference.* 5 vols., comp. George B. Stone. (New York: Pfizer, Inc, 1977).

"Sabin Oral Sundays in Cleveland." *Pfizer Scene* (June 1962): 6-7.

"Sharing the Care: Sharing the Medicine That Saves Lives." Pfizer pamphlet (1997). Pfizer archives.

Steere, William C. Alta Pharmaceuticals launch speech (March 3, 1998).

Steere, William C. Pfizer Employee's Day speech (July 23, 1998).

Steere, William C. Speech to American Society of Corporate Executives (March 14, 1998).

Steere, William C. "The Changing Pharmaceutical Marketplace and the Health Care Reform Debate." PMA Annual Meeting Speech (March 30, 1993).

Steere, William. C. Viagra launch speech (May 5, 1998).

Steere, William C. Vision and Mission speech (March 31, 1997).

Thackray, Arnold. Pfizer Oral History Project (1990-1994). Pfizer archives.

"Viagra: The Pill That's Changing the World — and Pfizer." *Pfizer Scene* (1998): 4-7.

Vision Statement (1997). Pfizer archives.

INDEX

A

Abbott, 75
Adams, Frank, 126
Advanced Candidate Management
    Team (ACMT), 121
Advocin, 104, 126
Agricultural Products Division, 104, 126
    founded, 85-86
    growth, 113
    products, research, 126
    (*see also* Animal Health Group)
Agrimycin, 86
Alitame, 126-127
Alta Pharmaceuticals, 139
Althius, Tom, 106
Amboise, France, 112
American Cyanamid, 89-91, 96
American Medical Systems, 125
American Society for
    Clinical Investigation, 56-57
amlodipine, 129
Anderson, George A., 35, 53-54, 66
    death, 107
    elected chairman, 69
    joined board, 29
Anderson, John, 24, 26, 35-36, 45
    appointed chairman, 29
    appointed general manager, 20
    company reorganization, 25
    consolidation of power, 27
    death, 53
    early career, 19
    resignation, 39, 41
angina, 120, 127
    (*see also* Procardia)
Animal Health Group:
    created, 104
    Revolution, 143-144
    SmithKline Beecham, 105, 143
    (*see also* Agricultural Products
    Division)
Anipryl, 143
anniversaries, 50, 89, 115, 148
Antarax, 119
anti-depression therapy, 140
    Zoloft, 128-129
Antibiotic Division, 85
Antibiotic Research Division, 81
Antivert, 95, 119
argols, 23, 29, 35, 40, 48
Aricept, 142
arthritis, 120-121, 142
ascorbic acid, 44
Aureomycin, 79, 89-90
Aviax, 104, 126

B

Bacacil, 120
Bachmann, Alex, 142
Banminth, 113
Barett, Brian, 143-145
Bargon, James, 121

Bartlett Street, 13-14
Beekman Street, 14
Bel-Jon, Nikos, 104
Bell, Alexander Graham, 18
BenGay, 51, 142
Bessey, Edward, 133
beta-thymidine, 127
Bi-con, 85
Bindra, Jasjit, 106
Blagg, J.C., 71
Bloom, Barry, 93, 110, 122, 136, 154
Board of Directors, 29, 146
bonus plan, 27
borax, 14, 18
Bowler, Ken, 137
Brady, Mathew, 16
Brandt, Peter, 123
Bright, Mike, 131-132
Bristol Laboratories, 90, 96
Bristol-Myers Company, 90-91, 124
Brooklyn Daily Eagle, 20
Brooklyn, New York operations,
    28, 33-34, 42, 52, 70, 125,
    150-151
    expansion, 64, 71
    fermentation of citric acid, 36-39
    first facility, 13
    penicillin production, 65, 68
Brown, Bob, 116
Brown, Michael, 147
Brunings, Karl, 82
Buerman, Carl, 71
Building 21, 38-39
Burns, Anthony, 147
Bush, George W., 142

C

calcium channel blockers, 120 (*see
    also* Procardia)
Camera Argumaria, 33
camphor, 14-15, 19-20
cardiovascular products, 116, 125
Carter, Anne Shirley, 62
Cefobid, 120, 123
Celebrex, 142
Centennial Award, 17
Central Research, 51, 106, 112-113,
    121-122, 129, 150-151
    Amboise, France, 112
    budget, 105, 119, 136
    commitment to, 109-110, 117,
        129, 136-137, 145, 151
    creation, 108
    Groton, Connecticut, 108, 110, 122
    Nagoya, Japan, 110-112
    risks, 145
    Sandwich, England, 93, 99, 109-
    111, 115
    (*see also* Research Division)
Chain, Ernest, 56
Charles Pfizer & Company, 25, 39,
    59, 84, 88, 91, 99-100, 103
    "Pfizer Quality" slogan, 17

accounting methods, 101-102
diversification, 96
emergence as pharmaceutical
    company, 80
expansion, 64, 69, 74
Export Division, 70
formation, 14
growth, 38, 51, 95
headquarters, 92
incorporation, 24
International Division, 51, 82-84,
    86, 95, 101-103, 105
losses, 24, 48
mission, 98
name change, 107
officers, 71
pioneer in use of telephone, 18
relocation, 70, 93
Cheirl, A.A., 32
Chemical Department, 38
Chemical Division, 126-127
Chemical Foundation, 35
*Chemical Trade Journal &
    Chemical Engineer*, 37
Chicago operations, 18-19
Chlorine Products Company, 23-24
chloroform, 15, 23-24
citrate of magnesia, 19
citric acid, 19, 33, 35, 69, 74
    fermentation, 50
    growth of, 23
    mass production, 30, 39, 45, 107
    prices of, 39
    uses, 18
Civil War, 15-16
Clemente, C.L., 123, 137, 150
Clinton, Hillary Rodham, 147
Clinton, William Jefferson, 133
Cochrane, T., 32
Collins, Gen. Lawton, J., 102
Columbia University, 60
Committee on Medical Research, 60
Communist Party, 45
Connors, Tom, 123
Conover, Lloyd, 110
Consumer Health Care Group, 51, 142
Consumer Products Division, 116, 126,
    135
Convexo-Concave heart valve, 125-126
Cooney, Tom, 108
Cornwell, W. Don, 147
Cortizone, 51, 142
Coty, 96, 126, 135
Cragwell, Gordon, 44, 57, 59
cream of tartar, 15, 48
    uses, 18
Currie, James, 30, 33, 35-36, 39,
    139

D

Davenport, John, 48, 57, 71, 94
Dawson, Martin, 56, 59
Deckert, Bill, 83

Dectomax, 104, 126, 143
deep-tank fermentation, 64-66
Deknatel's cardiovascular sutures, 125
Delmonico, Peter, 14
dental products, 115
Denzler, Harry, 48
Desitin, 51, 142
Desitin Chemical Company, 51
detailers, 84-85
diabetes, 119
Diabinese, 90, 93, 119
Diflucan, 124, 140
Diflucan One, 142
digestive disorders, 14
DNA, 118, 138-139
Dole, Bob, 140
Dombeck, Chuck, 123
Dow Chemical Company, 24
Drucker, Peter, 101-102
drug approvals, 95-96, 114
Drug Price Competition and Patent Restoration Act of 1984, 124
Drug Trade Club, 21
Duncan, Sir Oliver, 24

E

Early Candidate Management Team (ECMT), 121-122
Echt, Baron Bachofen von, 24
Erhart, Charles, 107, 151
    birth of children, 17
    death, 20
    early career, 13
    marriage, 14
    succession, 19
Erhart, Wilhelmine Klotz, 12
Erhart, William H., 24-25, 27, 29, 36, 41
    born, 17
    death, 53
    joins company, 19-20
Erythromycin, 130-131
EVE Award, 116

F

Federal Trade Commission (FTC), 88, 90
Feeney, Robert, 123
Feldene, 94, 104, 113, 119-121, 127
    piracy, 123
Fenton, Dick, 102, 103
Ferdinand, Archduke Francis, 29
fermentation technology, 30-31, 33, 35, 39, 44
    de-emphasis on, 112
    deep-tank, 39, 63
    surface, 59
Finlay, Alexander, 39, 71, 81
Fleming, Alexander, 55, 57, 60, 72
Florey, Lord Howard, 56
Food and Drug Administration (FDA), 96, 114, 116, 119-120, 124, 126-127, 140
Food, Drug, and Cosmetic Act, 95
Food Sciences Division, 135
Franklin Street, 18
Funk, Casimir, 44

G

General Agreement on Tariffs and Trade (GATT), 124
generic pharmaceuticals, 124-125
genetic manipulation, 138-139
Germany, Ludwigsburg, 13
Germany, Stuttgart, 17
gluconic acid, 39
Goett, Jack, 71
Goldmann, Randi, 121
Gordon Dryer machines, 35-36
Gray, Nigel, 115
Great Depression, 43-44
Groton, Connecticut, 50, 72-74, 76, 79, 106, 111-113, 125, 138
    Central Research, 108-110, 122
    expansion, 119, 122
    gene sequencing laboratory, 138
    Medical Research Laboratories, 93-94
    purchase, 73
    Terramycin production, 85

H

Hardwick, Chuck, 142
Harper, Forest, 142
Harper, Jo Anne, 145
Harvey, George B., 147
Hatch, Orrin, 124
Hausch, Anna, 15
Hayes, Arthur, Jr., 120
Heatley, Norman, 60
Hermes, 93
Hilton, Donald, 70, 82
Hobby, Gladys, 57, 59-60, 75, 81, 94
Hochstein, F.A., 82
Hoover, Herbert, 43
Horner, Constance J., 147
Hospital Products Group, 115, 125
Howmedica, 115-116, 125, 136

I

Ikenberry, Stanley O., 147
Intellectual Property Committee (IPC), 124
International Business Machines (IBM), 124, 146
International Centennial Exposition, 17
International Division, 51, 86, 95, 101-103, 105
    founded, 82-84
iodine, 14-15, 19, 35
Italian monopoly, 36, 39-40

J

Jackson, Bo, 125
Jake the dog, 144
Japanese operations, 111, 137, 140
Jaquet Fréres, 125
John L. Smith Cancer Research Center, 93-94
Johns Hopkins University, 60

Johnson & Johnson, 124
Johnston, David, 123
Jortner, Gary, 117
Jurassic Park, 138

K

Kamen, Harry P., 147
Kane, Jasper, 30, 33, 35, 39, 44, 47, 59, 64-65, 71, 81, 85, 107
Katen, Karen, 120, 123, 126, 137-138, 140, 144, 150
Keefer, Chester, 62
Kefauver, Estes, 90, 95, 102, 108
Kefauver-Harris Amendments, 95
Kelly, Pat, 132
Kemball-Bishop, 40, 45-46
Kennedy, Edward, 114
Koe, Ken, 129-130
Kolowsky, Donald, 126

L

Laboratorios Pfizer, S.A., 83
Labrecque, Thomas G., 147
Laubach, Gerald D., 103-104, 108, 112, 114, 133
    early career, 100
    resignation, 132
laxatives, 18-19
Lederle, 60, 75, 89
Leeming and Pacquin, 96
Lees, Tom, 81
Lend-Lease Act, 44
Levant wormseed, 14
Levin, Alan, 132
Lidoff, H.J., 90
Lilly, 75
Lipitor, 142
Liquamycin LA-200, 113
Littlejohn, Edward, 114
locations
    42nd Street, 93
    Amboise, France, 112
    Bartlett Street, 14
    Beekman Street, 14
    Building 21, 38-39
    Building 21A, 39
    Building 21B, 49
    England, 45, 93, 99, 109-113, 115, 120, 137
    Factory 12, 46
    Franklin Street, 18
    Maiden Lane, 14, 16, 19
    Marcy Avenue, 75
    Maywood, New Jersey, 93-94
    Niagara Falls, 23-24
    Nigeria, 101
    Ringaskiddy, Ireland, 125
    Vigo, 75
    (*see also* Groton, Sandwich, Nagoya, Amboise)
Loewe, Leo, 61, 63
Lombardino, Joseph, 120
Ludwigsburg, Germany, 13
Ludwigsburger Kreiszeitung, 13
Lull, Maj. Gen. George, 67
Luther, Herb, 85-86

M

MacTaggart, Barry, 110, 122-123
Mansil, 110-111, 120
Martin, Lynn, 116
Mathieson, Olin, 90
matrix management, 139
Matsuno, Soichi, 140
McClain, Dayle, 46-47, 71
McKeen, John, 39, 45-47, 59, 69, 74,
    77, 79, 82, 87, 89-90, 96, 101
    "5-by-5" sales goal, 95, 100
    death, 117
    retirement, 108
McKinnell, Henry A. Jr., 135,
    137, 140, 146
    career, 111, 150
    Medical Technology Group, 111
McMahon, J.R., 71
Mead, Dana G., 147
Mead, Frank, 48
measles, 95
Mecadox, 113
Medical Research Laboratories, 93
Medical Technology Group, 111, 115
Merck, 44, 57, 60-61, 75, 124
mercurials, 15
Meyer, Karl, 59
Micati, Victor, 112
Microbes, 143
Middlebrook, Bob, 83
Miller, Paul S., 114, 126, 150
Milne, George, 123, 136, 141
Mines, Samuel, 71
Minipress, 116, 119
Mitchell, John, 125
Morningstar-Paisley, 96
morphine, 15

N-O

Nagoya, Japan, 110-112
Naito, Haruo, 140
National Association for Research in
    Schizophrenia and Depression,
    130
National Defense Research Council,
    60
Navane, 119
Neimeth, Bob, 103
Niamid, 95
Niblack, John, 100, 121, 136, 146,
    150
Norvasc, 109, 113, 128, 131, 140
    discovery, 129
O'Connor, Hugh, 144
Oil, Paint & Drug Reporter, 53, 82
Olson, Laurie, 121
Oriental Importing and
    Manufacturing Company, 20-
    21
osteoarthritis, 120
over the counter medications, 142

P

P'an, S.Y., 79, 81
Parke-Davis, 75

Pasternack, Richard, 44, 71
Patelski, Ray, 71
patents, 124-125
Paul, Pope John II, 125
Payne Tariff Act, 27
penicillin, 51, 56-57, 69, 95, 98, 105,
    107
    "Penicillin fever," 60
    black market sales, 61
    Carter, Anne Shirley, 62
    demand for, 74
    discovery, 55-56
    early development of, 56-57
    media coverage, 62
    production, 58-60, 64-67, 69
    quality control department, 78
Penicillin chrysogenum, 59
Penicillium notatum, 55
Pfizer Canada, Ltd., 83
Pfizer Inter-American S.A., 83
Pfizer International Corporation, 83
Pfizer Pharmaceutical Group (PPG), 112,
    137-138, 146
Pfizer Quality slogan, 17
Pfizer Taito, 111
Pfizer, Alice, 16, 24-25
Pfizer, Anna, 16
Pfizer, Charles, 12, 107, 151
    death, 25
    early career, 13
    family, 14-16
    obituary, 25
Pfizer, Charles Jr., 16, 19-20, 24-
    25, 27
Pfizer, Emile, 16, 19, 24-25, 27, 29,
    36, 41, 53-54
Pfizer, Fanny, 14
Pfizer, Gustave, 16-17
Pfizer, Helen, 16, 24-25
Pfizer Inc, 110, 114, 117-119, 122-123,
    133, 136-137, 139
    Chemical Division, 126-127
    contributions to the world, 151
    emergence, multinational cor-
        poration, 108
    employee relations, 142
    expansion, 117, 119, 133, 138
    employee volunteer program,
        147
    intellectual property, 111, 117,
        123-124, 133
    logo, 107, 135
    Management Centers, 112
    name change, 107
    pharmaceutical focus, 144
    Pharmaceutical Steering
        Committee, 123
    philanthropic programs, 146
    streamlining, 123, 133, 137
    (*see also* Charles Pfizer &
        Company)
Pfizer, Johannes Jacob, 13
Pfizer, Karl Frederick, 13
Pfizer, Ltd., 83
Pharmacy Benefit Management
    Companies (PBMs), 145
pipeline concept, 100
Piper, Robert, 90

Piroxicam, 121
Plax, 126
Pliva Pharmaceuticals, 131-132
polio, 98-99
Powers, John J., Jr., 91, 101-104, 114,
    139, 146, 151
    "5-by-5" sales goal, 95
    early career, 71
    International Division, 82-84
    named president and CEO, 100
    Research Division, 99-100
    retirement, 108
Powers, John Sr., 55, 77
Powers Rx, 138-139
Pratt Pharmaceuticals, 129, 138
Pratt, Edmund T. Jr., 104, 108-
    116-117, 122, 138, 153
    consolidation of international
        and domestic, 103
    early career, 102-103
    investment in research, 103, 108-
        110, 112-113, 119
    patent protection, 117, 123-124
    retirement, 133
price fixing, 88-90, 97, 102
procaine hydrochloride, 74
Procardia, 120-121, 127
    sales, 120
Procardia XL, 104, 127
Proctor, Alan, 139
Proctor, Robert, 120
products
    Advocin, 104, 126
    Agrimycin, 86
    Alitame, 126-127
    Antarax, 119
    Antivert, 95, 119
    Aureomycin, 79, 89-90
    Aviax, 104, 126
    Bacacil, 120
    Banminth, 113
    BenGay, 51
    Beta-thymidine, 127
    Bi-con, 85
    Cefobid, 120
    Celebrex, 142
    Cortizone, 51
    Dectomax, 104, 126, 143
    Diabinese, 90, 93, 119
    Diflucan, 124
    Diflucan One, 142
    Liquamycin LA-200, 113
    Mansil, 111, 120
    Mecadox, 113
    Minipress, 116, 119
    Navane, 119
    Niamid, 95
    Reactine, 142
    RID, 51
    Rimadyl, 143
    Sigmamycin, 95
    Sinequan, 119
    Strep-combiotic, 69
    Streptomycin, 69, 75, 85-86, 151
    Tao, 95
    Terralac, 85
    Tetracyn, 50, 95
    Type I Sabin Oral vaccine, 99

Unasyn, 127
Unisom, 51
Vibramycin, 97, 119
Visine, 51
   (see also citric acid, Feldene,
   Norvasc, penicillin, Procardia,
   Procardia XL, tartaric acid,
   Terramycin, Terramycin LA,
   Zithromax, Zoloft, Viagra)
Prohibition, 33
Project Piglet, 85
Public Affairs Division, 114

Q-R

Queen's Award for Technological
   Achievement, 110-111
R&L Farms, 85
R&H Chemical Company, 23
Raines, Franklin D., 147
Raistrick, Harold, 56
Rangel, Charles, 137
Reactine, 142
Read, Ian, 144
Regna, Peter, 81
Research Division, 81, 91, 99
   advancements, 100
   facilities, 93-94
   (see also Central Research)
RespiSure, 143
rheumatoid arthritis, 120
Rhode Island, Newport, 25
riboflavin, 44
rickets, 44
RID, 142
Rimadyl, 143
Ringaskiddy, Ireland, 125
Robison, William "B.J.," 120, 129-130,
   132, 150
Roche, 44
rochelle salts, 18
Roerig Division, 120, 124, 126-127, 142
Roerig, J.B. and Company, 50
Rohatyn, Felix, 146
Routien, John B., 81
Royer, Bob, 102
Rubel Ice Plant, 65
Ryan, Herbert, 121

S

Sabin, Albert, 98-99
Said, Mohand Sidi, 144
Salk, Jonas, 99
Sandwich, England, 93-94, 99, 109-113,
   115, 126, 128
   Mansil, 111, 120
Saxton, Craig, 112
schistomiasis, 111, 120
Schmidt, Anne, 128
Schneider Medintag, 125
Schneider Worldwide, 136
scurvy, 44

Seeley, Don, 81
Senate Committee hearings, 90, 114
seratonin, 129, 131
Sharing the Care, 105, 146
Shedlarz, David, 150
Sherry's, 41
Shiley, Inc., 115, 125-126
Shino, Iwao, 111
Sigmamycin, 95
Simmons, Ruth J., 147
Sinequan, 119
Smith, Edwin, 102
Smith, John L., 32-35, 38-41, 43-48, 59,
   61, 63-67, 69, 73, 75, 77, 79-81
   death, 82
   named plant superintendent, 31
   work ethic, 33
SmithKline Beecham, 105, 143
Sobin, Ben, 76, 81
Société Anonyme pour le Commerce
   de tartre de France, 23
soil-screening program, 76-77, 111
   Terramycin development, 79
Solomons, I.A., 81
Sorin Biomedica, S.p.A., 126
Speciality Minerals Divisions, 135
Squibb (also E.R. Squibb & Sons), 31,
   57, 60-61, 75, 90, 96
Steere Pharmaceuticals, 139, 145
Steere, William C. Jr., 91, 117, 119, 122-
   134, 137, 140, 144, 146
   career highlights, 91, 104, 120
   education, 91
   State of the Business address, 148-149
   strategy in 1990s, 135
stock:
   initial public offering, 54
   splits, 54, 144
Stock, Fred, 75
Stockert Instruments, 125
Stone, George, 97
strategic alliances, 141
Streptomycin, 69, 75, 78, 85-86, 151
Stuart, Bill, 71
SUCIAC, 34-35, 40, 45, 69
   facilities, 38-39, 49
   first center of operations, 37
   impact on Pfizer, 38
sulfa drugs, 43

T

Taito Sugar Company, 111
Tanner, Ogden, 93
tartaric acid, 15, 18, 39
   "Operation Algeria," 40
   production, 15, 40
Teeter, Albert, 48
Telling, Fred, 123, 132
Terramycin, 50, 57, 60, 87-89, 93, 101,
   107, 109, 151
   agricultural applications, 85-86,
   113-114, 126

discovery, 79-80
International Division, 82-84, 95
patent, 81
private labeling, 80-81
testing, 79
Terramycin/LA, 113
tetracycline, 89-90, 96-97, 110
Tetracyn, 95, 101, 151
thoracic drainage devices, 125
Tompkins Streets, 13
trachoma:
   SAFE program, 147
   treatment, 146

U

U.S. Pharmaceuticals Group (USPG), 122
Uememura, Fred, 123
Unasyn, 127
Unisom, 51, 126, 142
Upjohn, 75, 90, 96

V

Vallès, Jean-Paul, 101, 133, 146-147
Valleylab, Inc., 125
Viagra, 105, 140
Vibramycin, 97, 100-111, 119
Victory Yard, 73
Vigo, 75-76, 86, 93
Vinson, J.W., 81
Visine, 51, 126, 142
vitamins, 43-44, 74
Voight, William, 23

W

W.R. Grace & Company, 101
Wallace, Mike, 130
Waxman, Henry, 124
Weaver, Herbert, 62
Weber, Ernst, 69, 75, 85
Weiner, Charles, 97
Welch, Willard, 129-130
Williamsburg, New York, 13, 19
Wiseman, Edward, 94, 120
Wizard of Oz campaign, 121
Woodward, Robert, 82
world headquarters, 104
World War I, 29-30, 35
World War II, 44, 49, 53, 55, 65, 67,
   69, 98
   Pearl Harbor bombing, 61
   postwar expansion, 73-74

Y-Z

yellow fever, 15
Zithromax, 113, 128, 129, 140, 146
   discovery, 130-132
Zoloft, 113, 128-129, 140
   discovery, 130-131